RAF Woodvale
The First
Fifty Years

Aldon P Ferguson

First published in 1991 by
Airfield Publications
18 Ridge Way
Wargrave
Berkshire RG10 8AS

© 1991 Text: Aldon P Ferguson
© 1991 Photographs various as shown

Printed by The Amadeus Press, Huddersfield

ISBN: 0 9511113 2 9

Meteor F8 VZ508 of No. 5 CAACU nicely positioned over RAF Woodvale in September 1971 just before the Meteors were retired from Woodvale. The photo clearly shows the extension to the main runway (04/22) at the northerly end built in 1951 and the pair of hangars on Main Site. The Meteor was flown by David Parker, Manager of Airwork Services Ltd. and the photograph taken by Squadron Leader A. Withington – Officer Commanding RAF Woodvale.

ROYAL AIR FORCE
WOODVALE
1941-1991

AUTHOR'S PREFACE

AN AIRFIELD is a living thing being planned for a specific function and evolving over the years to adapt to changing and challenging requirements. It is home to those stationed there; a hive of activity keeping aircraft and ancillary equipment serviceable and ready to undertake their respective tasks. It is a place of fun and enjoyment during off-duty times (and on-duty sometimes!) and sadness when an aircraft fails to return and its pilot lost.

RAF Woodvale was the first taste of leaving home to many young men and women in the early war years and always will remain part of their memories.

Woodvale was not a famous station and was just too late to help protect Merseyside in the 1940 Blitz. However it performed its function as a "Temporary" Royal Air Force Station, protecting Merseyside against German aircraft and U-Boats. It then changed to a support role which it has kept to this day. It is much smaller than its original form and houses a tiny fraction of the personnel and aircraft that were seen here in the forties and fifties. Today Woodvale supplies training and awareness of the RAF together with a prospering civil aviation function. This is the third History of RAF Woodvale that I have completed each greatly enhancing the previous and this edition has many new photographs and additional material. As can be seen from the text I am particularly short of information on the years 1944-46 and have no-ones personal memories of the Royal Navy occupation. If anyone can fill any gap or provide new information, however small, please contact the Author at the Publisher's address. Although only known by a few it is forgotten by none.

Aldon P Ferguson
Wargrave, Reading. June 1991

ROYAL AIR FORCE
WOODVALE
1941-1991
ACKNOWLEDGEMENTS

MANY, MANY people have helped me in my research into the story of RAF Woodvale and I have been particularly assisted by many of the Commanding Officers over my long connection with the base. In particular I would like to thank the following Commanders:

Group Captain J A McDonald; Squadron Leaders H G Boyne; A Withington; R J Gowring; M Schofield; M Redmore; P Jeffers; F C R Dicks; G Timms: M B Connell; K Lawry; R C Wright and G Clifford.

Many other Officers also helped and added to the story including Squadron Leader Norman Rose, Flight Lieutenants Steve Fisher; Trevor Jackson; Mike Kirk; Rod Newman; Kevin Long; Cliff Hilliker and many others. Flt Lt John (Deceased) and Connie Formby; Wing Commander T F Neil DFC⭑, AFC, AE, RAF Ret'd; Fred Chapman, one time Commanding Officer and Manager of Short Bros & Harland for many years; Group Captain H E Walmsley DFC; Squadron Leader R P Beamont CBE, DSO, DFC, FRAeS; Flight Lieutenant P Thornton Pett of the AHB; Sqn Ldr R T F Lyon CEng, MIMechE, AFRAeS, AMBIM; Wing Commander J R Turnbull and Squadron Leader Jim Wright.

No 611 Sqn R(Aux)AF Association, particularly Ken Reeves, Sam Prince and Ken Rice; Rev L Arridge BA; E Bell; Eric Bonser; E G Boulton; Don Brereton; Russell Brown, St Annes on Sea; Mrs M Butler; Phil Butler; Desmond Chorley; A Cook; Peter Corbell; Denis Corley; P A Cross; G F Culshaw; Ken Ellis; John Evans; Chas W Forster; Chris Foulds; Mr Hawthorne; John Hudson; Leslie Hunt; M A Kinnear; P G Knight; J W Jefferson; George Jones; Cliff Jessop; J Jones; M A Kinnear; K F Lillie; Stan Livesey; H Lloyd; Ken McCabe; Ian McConnochie; B McParlin; His Honour Deemster G E Moore; A B Musgrave; F J Neale; Mrs M Nickson; J W Orr; Arthur Pearcy Jnr, ARAeS; F Rawlings; E Rhodes; C Richardson; Brian Robinson; A Salvage; Mrs E Scragg; Mrs N Seabane; K T Sharples; Don Smith; Dave Smith; G Spinnell; E Stephenson; Ray Sturtivant; Mrs K E Trayford; Bryan Trunkfield; Dave Vernon; George Whitehead; Mrs Brenda Youlton; Neil Williams of the Liverpool Daily Post and Echo; the staff of the Public Records Office; and the team at the now defunct Merseyside Aviation Society who published the first two impressions of this book.

Mention must also be made of Stephenson Newspapers, Publishers of the Formby Times and Southport Visiter who have published much relating to Woodvale over the years. Refererces from Flypast (Journal of the Merseyside Aviation Society); Blitz over Merseyside (Published by the Liverpool Daily Post & Echo during the War); Liverpool Echo; Liverpool Daily Post; Air Pictorial; Flight International; FlyPast; The Royal Air Force Museum and Fighter Squadrons of the RAF and Coastal Support and Special Squadrons of the RAF both by John D R Rawlings.

A special thank you to Barry Abraham who took the time and patience to proof read the text for me and made several suggestions to keep me on the straight and narrow.

Sincere thanks to my patient wife, Sue, allowing me time behind the Word Processor and letting me off washing up and gardening to record the history of RAF Woodvale.

Finally, my apologies to anyone that I have missed out and thank you to all those who have served at RAF Woodvale for making a small part of the history of this unique Station.

The Main Sign at the entrance to RAF Woodvale announces the base and its units. *APF*

FOREWORD

RAF Woodvale was built as a Temporary Royal Air Force Station in 1941 for the defence of Merseyside during WWII. Initially, the Station consisted of 3 operational flying squadrons, a ground defence squadron, and 2 thousand personnel. This book relates the history of the airfield and lists the many units and aircraft types that have served at Woodvale. How the airfield has survived financial cuts during the last 50 years is a mystery, and, furthermore, as a non-established RAF Station it must be unique in todays Air Force. However, the future of the Station would now appear to be dependent on the future of the University Air Squadrons.

Recent implementation of a maintenance economy review has reshaped the Station, replacing the flying units accommodation and refurbishing all other buildings. With the resurfacing of the main runway and planned maintenance for operating surfaces, the airfield is well placed to continue supporting the RAF and civilian flying tasks.

This book is not an official history and opinions expressed do not necessarily represent the official position. With the detailed accuracy of an accomplished historian, Mr Ferguson has written a book that will give pleasure to all those interested in aviation or local history. His detail of the 50 years of RAF Woodvale will ensure that the memorable times are relived by some and understood by others.

R C WRIGHT
Squadron Leader
Officer Commanding
Royal Air Force Woodvale

Squadron Leader R.C. Wright, RAF. Officer Commanding RAF Woodvale since May 1988 standing in front of the list of MASUAS Commanding Officers.
Trinity Weekly Newspapers

Looking west from low level in 1943 showing the original Bellman hangar in the centre (since demolished) camouflaged runways and buildings. Two Tiger Moths can be seen beyond the hangar, a Dominie to the left and the top wing of the Swordfish immediately beyond – all belonging to No. 776 Squadron.

1943 aerial view of control tower looking west towards the coast. The letters 'OD' being war-time identification of Woodvale. The dispersals offices and blister hangar by the railway can be easily seen. Note the airfield map on the tower wall.

Genesis

BY SUMMER 1910 flying was well established at Freshfield beach, near Formby and Southport's response was to build a solitary hangar letting part of the sands to a garage proprietor named Woodhead, who believed he could attract wealthy flying men to his "aerodrome". The hangar was first occupied by a pioneer from Gargrave, near Skipton, named John Gaunt who was joined on 1st August 1910 by Grahame-White. Pioneer flying continued at Waterloo, Freshfield and Southport right up to the start of the First World War.

The expanse of sand at Southport was not forgotten by the military and an Aircraft Acceptance Park (AAP) was set up at Hesketh Park on the sand with two hangars built just back from the shore line in sand dunes. This unit accepted and assembled new aircraft and test flew them off the beach. The Vulcan factory in Crossens, Southport producing many for the Royal Flying Corps and Royal Naval Air Service (RFC & RNAS) and RAF.

After WWI the Southport (Hesketh Park Foreshore) Aerodrome as it was known became a licensed civil aerodrome with a sand landing area approx 880 square yards in diameter, mostly below the high water mark! The two hangars were available each being constructed of wood and metal measuring 80 ft wide, 170 ft long, 21 ft door height and 80 ft door width. It was operated by (GIROUX) Aviation Co who were to operate pleasure flights from Southport beach for about 50

years. A number of companies tried to link Southport to many centres of population including London, Manchester and Blackpool.

For WWII the hangars were taken back and pressed in military use with No 1 Packed Aircraft Transit Pool taking over, storing, assembling and delivering many aircraft such as Mosquitos, Spitfires, Tempests, Ansons, Albecores, Martinets and Waco gliders. In addition Martin Hearn Ltd of Hooton Park used these buildings for repair and overhaul of aircraft.

Post war it reverted to civilian use, was taken over by Southport Corporation as a bus depot and the hangars were eventually demolished in the 1960s.

Birkdale Sands maintained the flying link with Southport since WWII with a sand airfield activated every year for pleasure flights. For many years operated by Giroux aviation in Fox Moths and more recently with Cessna 172s.

The flat land around Southport made excellent natural airfield country and was searched out by Air Ministry site finders in the early days of WWII.

Major Joseph Schmid, Head of Luftwaffe Intelligence, wrote in a paper entitled "Proposal of the Conduct of Air Warfare against Britain" in November 1939. It started:-

"The most important ports must be attacked without exception and as far as possible simultaneously. The intermixture of residential areas with dockyards in some British ports is no reason for failing to attack such ports. The

Taken on 20 August 1942 for camouflage effectiveness purposes this photo clearly shows the outline of the original fields and large areas of sand. All the buildings and runways are painted but the main road remains a valuable reference point for the Luftwaffe.   *RAF Museum*

most important ports are those of London, LIVERPOOL, Hull, Bristol and Glasgow. In all of these ports their primary target will be shipping. As secondary targets dockyards and warehouse installations, in particular food and oil stores and silos, may be attacked. To achieve the maximum effect, even small formations may be usefully employed."

On 29 November 1939 Hitler issued his Directive No 9 "Instructions for warfare against the economy of the enemy" and the concept of the Blitz on Britain was born. The air raid sirens sounded on Merseyside on the night of 25 June 1940 (just before the Battle of Britain began) and aircraft were heard over the city. However, the night was cloudy and no bombs fell. Over a month passed before any bombs fell in the Liverpool district and no serious damage was inflicted until late August. On the night of 28 July 1940 three high explosive (HE) bombs fell near a searchlight post at Altcar, near Formby; several more dug craters on the Wirral and on 1 August several dropped on Halewood, south of Liverpool. The first fatality was Joanna Mandale, a domestic servant in Prenton Lane, Prenton, Birkenhead, who lost her life when a bomb struck the roof of her house at 12.30 am on 9 August. The following night more bombing killed seven in Wallasey and during the next few nights enemy aircraft laid mines in the Mersey estuary for the first time.

Liverpool had its first bombs around midnight on 17 August falling in the Caryl Street area. There was damage to the overhead railway and a shed, but a block of tenements was undamaged by a bomb which made a large crater in the road nearby. Between August 1940 and May 1941, 3,966 people lost their lives and 120,000 houses were damaged in Liverpool - what of the defences?

The North of England was unprepared for enemy air attacks. The Luftwaffe realised that day attacks would lead to unacceptable casualties and also that the Royal Air Force had only primitive radar for night interception. Defence of the Merseyside area fell on the nearest RAF stations at Speke (the civil airport requisitioned for the RAF); Squires Gate at Blackpool (also requisitioned); Cranage, near Middlewich; Tern Hill, near Market Drayton, Shropshire; Valley in Anglesey and Ringway, South of Manchester, all operating within No 12 Group, Fighter Command.

A hurried ring of anti-aircraft guns and searchlights were provided around Liverpool and Manchester but at that time there was no radar, range-finding for prediction and accuracy was limited relying on visual gun-sights.

No 9 Group, Fighter Command was formed at Barton Hall, near Preston, on 1 September 1940 becoming operational on 2 October and having Speke; Baginton, near Coventry; Jurby (Isle of Man) and Tern Hill as its Sector stations for the defence of the North West of England. The first operational squadron was No 312 (Polish) Squadron at Speke with Hurricanes but by August 1941 Cranage (Cheshire), High Ercall (Shropshire), Valley (Anglesey), Atcham (Shropshire), Honiley (Warwickshire), Llanbedr (Merionthshire) and Squires Gate (Lancashire) had been added to its fighter stations.

None of the aircraft operated from these stations had any form of radar or homing aids and relied on ground controllers and the Observer Corps spotters to be guided onto their targets. The Hurricanes at Speke were essentially day fighters

Also taken in August 1942 the general arrangement of Woodvale can be clearly seen together with the Cheshire Lines Railway in the top right. Dispersals were constructed along the Liverpool – Southport railway side and to the south of the airfield. The edge of the communal site can be seen extreme bottom right.
RAF Museum

and saw very little action against the raiders. The squadrons away from the immediate environment fared better being able to gain height whilst making for Liverpool but relied on the searchlights and glow from the fires for the identification of the Heinkel He 111, Dornier Do 17 or Junkers Ju 88 bombers. Considering that over three hundred bombers were over Merseyside on some nights from August 1940 to May 1941 the interception rate was appalling and totally unacceptable to both the RAF and public morale.

Speke, Cranage, Tern Hill and Squires Gate all had grass runways and even had difficulty in getting their aircraft airborne in wet weather. Therefore early in 1941 it was decided to build a new all weather airfield to take the pressure off these other airfields and be responsible for the defence of Merseyside. Several areas were considered but the flat farm land to the South of Southport was considered to be the best with the advantages of access to a main road (A565) and railway at Woodvale Station on the Cheshire Lines Railway. The land was occupied to the North by Bronk and New Bronk Farms and to the South by the Liverpool Merchant Bank and Insurance Golf Club. The area was free from trees and contained very few houses.

Work started immediately and it was designed on the typical three runway lay-out to allow aircraft to take off and land as much as possible into wind. The technical site was located adjacent to the dual carriageway (Built just before 1939), at the Woodvale end of the airfield utilising the existing road to the two farms. The main runway (04-22) was laid parallel to the Liverpool to Southport railway line, a decision being dictated by the longest available run and not the prevailing wing direction (south-west). Three Bellman hangars were erected with a standard control tower (Ref 12779/41), brick offices and workshops, stores, parachute store and armoury, whilst hardstandings for forty-one aircraft were arranged around the perimeter track. Eight steel blister hangars were erected around the perimeter as were the dispersed fuel and explosive stores. Being a fighter station, no bomb dump was ever built. On the west side of the dual carriageway several fields were requisitioned for the erection of the Communal Site incorporating the Officers' Mess, Sergeants' Mess, Airmens Institute, NAAFI etc. Seven living sites were constructed each capable of accommodating over one hundred airmen, two WAAF sites including a WAAF mess, the Operations Block and, finally, the Station Sick Quarters around Hall Farm on the Old Southport Road. The living accommodation was in timber huts with pitched roofs and felted walls and roofs.

Thus a small town developed capable of accommodating over two thousand airmen and airwomen together with their officers, plus being able to operate three squadrons simultaneously and looking after their operations, repair, routine maintenance etc.

Although far from complete and with only one runway operational and accommodation still under construction, Squadron Leader R A Marwick was posted to RAF Woodvale from RAF Speke for administrative duties assuming command of the Care and Maintenance Party responsible for the opening up of a new fighter station on 25 October 1941. They were accommodated in Southport as no buildings were yet ready for occupation. The immediate job was to hasten construction and get the airfield ready for its first squadron. The winter weather did not assist but on 24 November Station Headquarters (now the Officers Mess) and part of the main stores were taken over and equipped ready to receive equipment which was now arriving in large consignments. The first Station Commander, Group Captain J A McDonald visited from his current command at RAF Speke on 27th for an inspection. The guard-

room and one squadron office were taken over on 2 December and a temporary Officers' Mess opened in the now defunct Golf Club House at the Freshfield end of the base. On the same day two sergeants huts and four airmens huts were taken over on Site No 5 whilst two officers huts were also handed over.

Personal memories of the first few days give an insight into life on an unfinished RAF station. Many of the airmen were posted in from Speke but even at the end of 1941 the station was not properly functioning and gate guard was provided by two elderly civilians. There was an establishment for eight RAF police, later reduced to six with a Flight Sergeant in charge. There was no sentry box for six months but a continuous guard was mounted at the main gate. Opposite the gate were crated aircraft on the central reservation of the dual carriageway where they could be guarded before going to Hesketh Park, Southport for assembly and test flying. Guards were posted at each hangar and in the control tower at night and the freezing winter of 1941/2 is still remembered! In the WAAF billets there were 26 girls to a room and in the RAF billets the water was frozen and the only way to wash was to break the ice from the surrounding ditches and heat it up if possible. The WAAFs had breakfast and dinner in their own mess but it was too far away from the airfield to return to for lunch. The WAAFs were ferried by lorry to and from work but the airmen had to either walk or use the service bicycles which were issued.

WAAF Communal Site with the airfield top right. RAF Sites Nos. 1 and 7 can be seen top centre and top right respectively.

First Squadron

THE FIRST daily routine orders were issued on 10 December and the advance party of No 308 (Polish) Squadron arrived from RAF Northolt. The airmen were to occupy No 3 Site whilst the officers and aircrew were accommodated in either the Golf Club House or billeted out in Formby. The Squadron had enjoyed a successful tour at Northolt, west of London but was involved in heavy fighting losing many aircraft and pilots. It was notified in November that it would move to Woodvale but due to delays in completion of the airfield the move was postponed. The Squadron moved by train taking a whole day. The ground crew arrived in darkness and learned the worst. Group Captain Pawlikowski told the pilots that conditions were worse than Russia or Tobruk, but at least they could draw field rations! Sand was everywhere, heating hardly existed and water had not yet been laid on to many of the dispersed sites. On 13 December the Commanding Officer, Squadron Leader Wesolowski went to Speke to see Group Captain J A McDonald to complain about conditions. The Squadron's Spitfire II's were delivered into Speke and six were flown to Woodvale on 13th being the first aircraft to land at Woodvale. On 14th the aircraft were tested and inspected. The feeling of revolution collapsed as the Squadron slowly became organised and established in its new home; one flight became operational. On 15th the Squadron was at readiness and undertook its first sector reconnaissance.

Woodvale was now a Sector Station in No 9 Group, RAF Fighter Command. The Operations Room in Broad Lane was not yet completed therefore a school at Aughton Springs, Halsall, about five miles to the East of the Station, was taken over and temporarily fitted out as an Operations Room. Group Captain J A McDonald was Sector Commander and was based at Speke until 15 January 1942 when he arrived at Woodvale and assumed command. The Woodvale Sector was responsible for the defence of Merseyside and controlled the area including Manchester, Liverpool, Preston, Lancaster and part of North Wales.

During their first week at Woodvale, No 308 Squadron undertook training flights and several pilots went to RAF Squires Gate as work was still continuing on Woodvale's runways. On 17th practice interceptions were made over Preston whilst a note in the Squadron Official record Book (RAF Form 540) states that the newer pilots went to Squires

Grave of Pilot Officer Krawczynski and Squadron Leader M.J. Wesolowski both of 308 (Polish) Squadron, at Our Lady's Church of Compassion, Formby. *APF*

Gate as the runways at Woodvale were not yet safe.

The first fatality occurred on 21 December, when Pilot Officer E Krawczynski, aged 28, crashed in his Spitfire II with its nose being buried deep into sand in the Ribble Estuary, half a mile South of Lytham. It is assumed that his engine failed and that he died in the resultant forced landing. He was buried at Our Lady's Church in Formby with full military honours.

No 308 Squadron were using their stay at Woodvale to rest, re-equip and train ready to return to the more active fighting in No 11 Group's area in the South of the country. However, they also acted as defence for Merseyside and the Woodvale sector although by the time the airfield became operational the bombing threat to the area from the Luftwaffe had evaporated.

Six new officers and eight new NCO pilots arrived with

Woodvale Station and Squadron senior personnel 1942. Front row left to right Flight Lieutenent Neiper, ? , Squadron Leader Hartley, Wing Commander T.N. Haynes (OC256 Squadron.), Group Captain J.A. McDonald (Station Commander), Group Captain Bowling, Wing Commander J.S. Adams (256 Squadron.), Squadron Leader Miksa (OC 315 (Polish) Squadron.), Squadron Leader Markham, Squadron Leader G.E. Moore (Station Adjutant). *G.E. Moore*

Group Captain J.A. McDonald (right) in conversation with Group Captain Broughall to whom he was handing over control of RAF Speke.

Group Captain McDonald

the Squadron on 29 December but facilities were not good enough for training, even using Squires Gate, and they were sent to another squadron. Discussions were held with No 285 Squadron at Squires Gate regarding night fighting and searchlight co-operation but little night flying was undertaken by No 308. On 19 December Wing Commander G D Pinkerton, DFC arrived to take over command of the station from Squadron Leader Marwick who had been in command since October, but he only commanded for four weeks pending the arrival of Group Captain McDonald on 15 January 1942. The Air Officer Commanding (AOC) Fighter Command visited on 3 January but his visit was marred by a fatal accident involving three of the Squadron's personnel; Sergeant Hill, Corporal Lesniak and Leading Aircraftman (LAC) Gawlik. They were in an RAF lorry conveying men back to work from the living sites when it was involved in a crash with a double decker bus. It occurred on the Old Southport Road close to the Freshfield roundabout and four others were seriously injured and taken to hospital. This accident resulted in a fifteen miles per hour speed restriction being put on all vehicles within the station bounds except for ambulances and crash vehicles in cases of emergency.

The Squadron scrambled its readiness flight on 5 January but no enemy aircraft were seen and two days later two aircraft were sent to RAF Valley for gunnery practice. A dawn patrol on 9th resulted in another fatal accident when the CO, Squadron Leader M J Wesolowski, aged 28, collided with Flying Officer Dolicher, his Spitfire going down in a spin, crashing and killing him outright. Dolicher managed to regain control and landed safely at Woodvale. Permission was received on 11th to bury part of Pilot Officer Krawczynski's body with the CO and they were buried at Our Lady's Church, Formby, on 13 January.

The first section of WAAFs arrived on 12 January consisting of telephone operators, cooks and clerks, occupying their newly completed accommodation in North Moss Lane. Weather was unfit for flying so the Squadron's pilots went to Speke for link trainer sessions. Squadron Leader Nowierski arrived to take over command of the Squadron on 18 January but two days afterwards the station was completely snowed in. Five hundred men and three snow ploughs were kept busy all day attempting to clear the runways which came back into operation well in advance of expectations. Heavy rain on 24th cleared away the remaining snow and flying was resumed. The

Squadron was now able to vacate its temporary accommodation in a farmhouse and take over purpose built offices. 26 January saw the start of the Squadron re-equipping with Spitfire Vb's with four arriving and by 30th there were fourteen on strength. Another scramble took place on 5 February, the section being vectored to the Point of Air but no enemy aircraft were seen. On the same day the Squadron was able to take over its newly completed hangar although the aircraft were usually dispersed at the hardstandings unless undergoing maintenance.

New Bronk Farm was located adjacent to the Liverpool to Southport railway line whilst Bronk Farm house was immediately to the North of where the control tower is currently located. Both farms were requisitioned and their buildings taken over as temporary accommodation. The farm house and their barns remaining until well after the end of WWII and the barn to Bronk Farm being used as the fire section garage up to 1991 but at the time of writing is due for demolition with a new section building replacing it. Sites 5 and 6 were taken over on 13 January, the PBX building on 14th, parachute store on 8 February and the WAAF Officers Mess, NAFFI and living quarters on 16th.

The first real action took place on 11 February when Flying Officer Dolicher and Sergeant Marek were scrambled to intercept a Ju 88 over Lancaster at twenty thousand feet. The section was handicapped as it was flying the older Spitfire II's as the new breeches had not yet been fitted to the Vb's. The section intercepted the Ju 88 but it took evasive action into cloud, limiting the line of attack the section could take. The enemy aircraft was hit and left with its port engine smoking, however the Spitfires ran out of ammunition and had to return to base, both landing safely and claiming one probable.

War-time austerity was beginning to bite – a pig farm was set up and the pigs arrived on 20 February. The local farms were great producers of asparagus in the sandy soil and several crops of asparagus were yielded. Also a programme of various garden and vegetable plots on the airfield was instigated to supplement rations. In March it was decided that Sunday was to become a normal working day. WAAF were allowed one day off a week whilst airmen and officers only half a day. Station transport was similarly reduced and airmen had to walk from their dispersed living quarters whilst the WAAF were still transported. By early March No 3 Site was completed and No 1 WAAF Site started.

New Bronk Farm House remained adjacent to the control tower until the early 1950's providing additional accomadation for radio repairs. The map on the tower wall was covered after WWII and only rediscovered in the late 1970's when it was reinstated. Photo dated 1943.

Main Gate 1943 with two sentry boxes, one to each side, guard room immediately to the right again. Domestic fire station to the left of the gate and PBX Building mid left. Note bushes and trees long since removed.

9 February was a hectic day with two sections on patrol but with no encounter. The CO, Squadron Leader Nowierski, was driving two squadron officers to Liverpool when they were involved in an accident. The CO and Plt Offs Pictruiski and Ilioski were taken to Southport Emergency Hospital with cuts but no serious injuries. The CO returned to flying two days later. An unusual occurrence happened on 13 February when the Squadron was engaged in a mock dog fight. Fg Off Paley baled out of his aircraft, landing safely by parachute. When questioned he admitted that there had been nothing wrong with his aircraft but he went into a black-out and only regained consciousness when he found himself in a parachute falling to earth. The record does not mention the repercussions at the Court of Inquiry!

The following day a section of four aircraft was scrambled to go to Kirton-in-Lindsay to practice reinforcing that side of the sector. On 18th there were three scrambles without result but another aircraft was lost when Fg Off Kudrawicz force landed the Squadron's Miles Magister training aircraft when its engine failed.

A scramble on 21 February resulted in another interception when Sergeants Zielinski and Marecki were directed to Lancaster. At fourteen thousand feet they spotted a Ju 88 at eighteen thousand feet travelling in a northerly direction. The enemy aircraft turned west and the section closed in. Zielinski closed to four hundred yards when the enemy top and lower rear gunners opened fire, Zielinski replied closely followed by Marecki. The enemy aircraft dived for cloud and on emerging Zielinski closed to two hundred yards giving short bursts with cannon and machine guns until all his ammunition was exhausted, by this time he noted that the rear gunner had stopped firing. One of Zielinski's cannons had jammed and he went over the enemy aircraft with the intention of cutting its tail off, whilst doing this he prevented Marecki from firing and owing to background noise on the R/T he was unable to contact Zielinski. The Junkers managed to get into some cloud and make off. A claim of one damaged Ju 88 was filed. On landing Zielinski discovered bullet holes in his starboard wing. The action took place over Walney Island at about 12.45 and the Squadron was credited with a damaged aircraft.

By March 1942 Woodvale had been completed with the exception of finishing the dispersed sites to the East side of the dual carriageway where water and electricity was still restricted. No 3 Site had been taken over on 13 March and the Technical Block, dispersal buildings and Flight Offices were taken over on 20 April. During January a barber's shop had opened on the Communal Site but was restricted to daylight hours because no electricity was available. There was initially some friction between the British and Polish Officers and they were separated before the purpose-built Officers' Mess was completed on the Communal Site. The Polish used the old Golf Club House at the Freshfield end of the airfield whilst the British were accommodated in Cavendish House, a large Victorian house located just north of the airfield on the other side of the A565 adjacent to Woodvale Railway Station. This was located to the North east of the junction of the A565 and the Coast Road where the traffic lights are today.

Unfortunately, Woodvale was built too late to have any effect against the main blitz on Liverpool. There was the occasional "Flash" raid by lone or pairs of enemy bombers flying low to avoid detection. Such raids strafed Green Lane in West Derby, streets in the centre of Woolton and a bus and streets in Speke. Woodvale was under construction at the time and there were only seven more raids after 8 May 1941 - most of them quite ineffective. The last bombs of all, a stick of four, demolished five houses in Upper Stanhope Street, Liverpool, on the night of 10 January 1942 killing fifteen people. These attacks were at night and beyond the scope of No 308 Squadron who had to leave the interceptions to No 156 Squadron from Squires Gate and No 96 Squadron at Cranage.

The Russian offensive had commenced and the bombers of Luftflotte 3 were diverted two thousand miles to the East where their luck ran out. In the blitz on Liverpool their loss rate had only been one per cent and there is no doubt that if they had persisted the damage to the City and Port would have been on an entirely different scale. No 308 Squadron certainly helped to protect the Port and was efficient at dissuading reconnaissance aircraft flying up the Irish Sea. Training flights continued in early March with a station defence exercise held on 7th and a scramble for convoy protection on 28th. On 8 March, one of the Squadron's pilots, Flying Officer Poplawski, was notified that he had been awarded the highest Polish decoration, the Virtuti Militard for his bravery whilst the Squadron was flying from Northolt.

Defence Flight HQ in foreground with MT Section centre and firing-in butts beyond. Original Bellman hangar top left with tower just visible top left. 1943.

Second Polish Squadron –
First Kill

THE RE-EQUIPPING and resting of the Squadron was almost complete, Fg Off Dolicher was posted to No 56 Operational Training Unit (OTU) as an instructor and four new pilots were posted in straight from an OTU on 10 March. The Squadron was advised that they were to move to Exeter on 31 March. Flying continued with a reinforcement exercise to Valley on 29th but the advance party left on 28th and the advance party of the replacing squadron, No 315 (Polish), arrived on the same day to prepare for their arrival. The 30th was spent packing, saying farewell to local friends and a special train was loaded at Woodvale station. Two Harrow transport aircraft arrived to ferry the mechanics to Exeter so that the Squadron could remain operational immediately after arrival. The train left on 31st but due to bad weather the Squadron's Spitfires could not leave until 2 April when all fifteen aircraft flew back to the air fighting war. Air Vice Marshal Sir W McClaughtry, CB, DSO, AFC, AOC No 9 Group, Fighter Command, based at Barton Hall Preston, visited to say farewell to No 308 and welcome his new fighter squadron, No 315. No 4 Site had been taken over only five days earlier and at last completion was in sight.

No 315 (Polish) Squadron was also at RAF Northolt and had similarly suffered during the Battle of Britain requiring rest and re-training. Its last operational sortie with No 11 Group was on 28 March providing top cover for a raid on France but no enemy aircraft were sighted. Squadron Leader Janus brought the Squadron and its Spitfire Vb's to Woodvale on 1 April, taking off for a sector recce on 2nd and having their first scramble in the afternoon when one section was ordered to patrol over the sea near Blackpool. After orbiting for twenty minutes they were recalled. On 5 April Red and Yellow sections were airborne to provide cover for convoy "Topaz" but due to confusion with the controllers the convoy was not found. Convoy patrols were one of the duties given to Woodvale squadrons – searching them out either in or out bound from Liverpool and providing cover against enemy air attack in addition to spotting for enemy submarines.

Squadron Leader Janus was awarded a second bar to his Polish decoration for bravery "Krzyz Walecznych" on 6 April.

In a parade at the main gate in 1942 a Polish Guard of Honour presents arms for the arrival of the Station Commander, Group Captain J.A.McDonald, followed by Air Vice Marshall Ujejski. The corner of the guard room can be seen to the right. *Group Captain J.A.McDonald*

315 (Polish) Squadron Spitfire Vb's taxi-ing across the grass after a sortie in 1942. *Group Captain J.A. McDonald*

Twelve Spitfires of No. 315 Squadron in practice formation over Woodvale in 1942. *Group Captain J.A.McDonald*

Flying continued as it did with No 308 Squadron; one section was always on readiness during daylight hours whilst the remainder of the Squadron undertook convoy patrols, air firing practice with Blackburn Roc and Skua aircraft of No 776 Squadron at Speke, exercises with searchlight batteries and occasionally a section would be called to Valley to provide extended cover for a convoy. A note in the ORB states "How the sand blows here! – but grass seeding was in hand and the oncoming spring was hoped to cure it. However sand was to be a constant problem.

A detachment of No 285 Squadron arrived on 14 April and took over a newly completed dispersal near to the railway line. The Squadron had its headquarters at RAF Wrexham and operated detachments at Honiley and Squires Gate. Flying Officer Reynolds who was in charge of the detachment was ordered to fly his one Oxford and two Defiants to Woodvale. The detachment was supported by twenty airmen and three sergeant pilots. It provided army co-operation in the Woodvale sector devoted to training all gun batteries, gun laying and Ground Controlled Interception (GCI) crews. They were also to provide towed targets for practice shoots. Most of the flying was to be undertaken by day but also by night subject to twenty four hours notice. Over the year the strength of the detachment grew as it became responsible to more gun batteries including:

Woodvale from the north west corner of the airfield, Liverpool/Southport railway across bottom, blister hangar bottom right and Main Site in centre. *1943.*

33 Brigade Mersey
44 Brigade Manchester
53 Brigade Formby
70 Brigade West Derby
58 Brigade Crewe

No 315 Squadron was still on readiness and on 3 May Blue Section was scrambled taking off at 06.40. Blue Two had engine trouble and an uneventful patrol but Blue One, Pilot Officer Stembrawicz, in Spitfire AB241, was vectored onto a Ju88. After manoeuvring above the "hun" he was able to attack with cannon and machine gun fire and as a result of the first pass black smoke poured from the port engine of the enemy aircraft. Stembrawicz gave chase firing as the opportunity occurred, his last burst being at about fifty yards. The Ju88 was losing height rapidly and was last seen just above the sea. Stembrawicz followed to within about six feet of the water but was forced to break away because he was out of ammunition and low on fuel. The aircraft was claimed as destroyed – the first by a Woodvale based aircraft.

Flight Lieutenant Reynolds and pilots of No. 285 Squadron posing by one of the detachments Oxfords shortly after their arrival in April 1942. *John Hudson*

The following day was National Polish Day and duly celebrated, but convoy patrols continued. Squadron Leader Janus passed over command of the Squadron to Squadron Leader Wiorkiewicz on 6 May who arrived from Northolt where he had taken part in more than thirty sorties over enemy occupied territory. May and June passed quietly with the Squadron providing continuous daylight cover for the Sector. The readiness section being scrambled on 30 May, 3, 5, 19, 24 and 27 June but with no sightings. The Luftwaffe vertical reconnaissance photograph illustrated in this book was taken from very high altitude on 5 May 1942 and it is interesting to note that whilst the Squadron was scrambled on that day there is no mention of any enemy aircraft sighted by anyone at Sector control. The shortcomings of the system are highlighted as an enemy aircraft was able to fly directly overhead and not even be seen. It was obviously a very clear day but the aircraft was somewhere between 15,000 and 20,000 ft and its engines would have been almost inaudible.

On 16 May 1942 five officers of No 776 Squadron (Fleet Air Arm) arrived from Speke as the advance party of the Squadron which was to retain its headquarters at Speke but undertake most of its flying from Woodvale. The detachment arrived a few days later with a mixture of Rocs, Skuas, Chesapeakes and a Dominie for communications. The unit's role was a Fleet Requirements Unit (FRU) providing aircraft to act as targets or target tugs for calibration and practice of ships

Members of No 285 Squadron around a Defiant in a sand-bag constructed dispersal revetment in 1942. Front row left to right: Flight Sergeant Burgess, Flight Sergeant Knight, Flight Lieutenant Reynolds (detachment Commander), Warrant Officer Hedge, ?, far right in sweater John Hudson. *John Hudson*

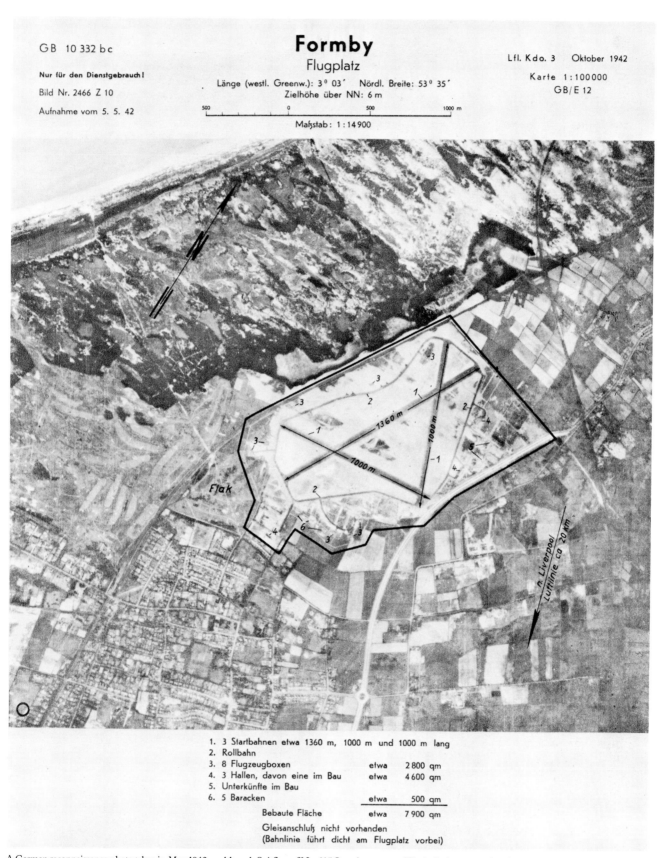

Formby
Flugplatz

Länge (westl. Greenw.): 3° 03′   Nördl. Breite: 53° 35′
Zielhöhe über NN: 6 m

Maßstab: 1 : 14 900

Lfl. Kdo. 3   Oktober 1942

Karte 1 : 100000
GB/E 12

Flak

1360 m

1000 m

1000 m

n. Liverpool
Luftlinie ca 20 km

1. 3 Startbahnen etwa 1360 m, 1000 m und 1000 m lang
2. Rollbahn
3. 8 Flugzeugboxen   etwa   2 800 qm
4. 3 Hallen, davon eine im Bau   etwa   4 600 qm
5. Unterkünfte im Bau
6. 5 Baracken   etwa   500 qm

    Bebaute Fläche   etwa   7 900 qm

Gleisanschluß nicht vorhanden
(Bahnlinie führt dicht am Flugplatz vorbei)

A German reconnaissance photo taken in May 1942 − although Spitfires of No. 315 Squadron were at Woodvale the enemy aircraft was not spotted. Named 'Formby' by the Luftwaffe, Woodvale is shown with eight blister hangars, three Bellman hangars and Flak! As far as it is known Flak never existed at Woodvale. No mention is made of the dispersed living site.

APF

No. 256 Squadron on a Beaufighter, in front of one of Woodvale's Bellman hangars, after it moved from Squire's Gate in June 1942. *G.A. Peakman*

anti-aircraft gun defences or any other Royal Naval Unit in the area. The Royal Navy took over the holiday Lido on Ainsdale beach and developed it into a gunnery school known as HMS Queen Charlotte (a "Stone Frigate"). This unit had a series of guns facing the open sea and aircraft of the FRU would trail targets or dive-bomb the school to give the gunners practice. The targets were either drogues looking like wind-socks or small model aircraft, mostly manufactured by the toy firm, Tri-ang.

Now that the dispersals were ready for occupation, the technical block, dispersals, dispersal buildings and flight offices were all taken over from the contractors on 20 April, there was now room for more units. As Woodvale was the sector station, No 256 Squadron was moved from Squires Gate on 4 June 1942 with a mixture of Defiants, Blenheims and Beaufighters. The Squadron had been at Squires Gate since March 1941 flying Defiant I's converting onto Defiant II's in October 1941 and also receiving some Blenheims and slowly converting onto Beaufighters. This Squadron had borne the brunt of the defence of Merseyside during the blitz and had several enemy aircraft to its credit. It had been supported by No 96 Squadron which was based on the grass airfield at Cranage near Middlewich, Cheshire. The move to Woodvale was logical as it allowed one station to provide 24 hour cover and it was under the control of the Sector Commander, Group Captain MacDonald. The move also took away the operational requirement from Squires Gate and allowed it to concentrate on it's training role as well as test flying Wellington bombers.

"A" Flight flew across the Ribble estuary to Woodvale, followed by "B" Flight two days later together with the CO, Wing Commander J S Adams, The first incident occurred only a few days later on 8th when Sergeant J T Walker successfully landed on one engine on his first solo in a Blenheim. The engine cut whilst over Squires Gate and shortly before reaching Woodvale the prop of the u/s engine tore loose and broke away.

Woodvale now housed two fighter squadrons, No 256 and No 315, together with the majority of No 776 Squadron and the detachment of No 285 Squadron. By 11 June three blister hangars had been completed and were handed over to No 256 Squadron. No 256 was up to full strength with Beaufighters by 23 July and on 12 August carried out a mock

attack on Valley with No 315 Squadron which was highly successful, Valley being officially wiped out! No 256 had a "very wet and enjoyable" party in the Lighthouse Cafe at Formby on 20 August and undertook evening patrols on almost every other night during the month but with no enemy contact.

No 315 Squadron lost another pilot on 19 July 1942 when Sergeant Pilot Tadeusz Nawrocki failed to return from a sortie in Spitfire Vb W3628. Neither the Squadron nor the Station records even mention this fact but it became known due to his grave in Our Lady of Compassion churchyard in Formby. Desmond M Chorley from Agincourt, Canada became interested in the story in 1981 and researched the accident and the pilots family. The reason for the accident is unknown but Desmond actually found an eye witness of the accident – 39 years after the tragic event. A Mr T E W Carford from Morecambe wrote "I was in the Army stationed at Lunecliffe, a large house two miles south of Lancaster, at the time. I saw the plane flying quite low, I was standing in the enclosure outside the building and watched it, about 30 yards away. It hit the top of some trees and then flew straight up in the air and then bounced down in a field and then into the edge of the A588 road, which runs along the side of Lunecliffe, at the same time it hit a cattle truck and immediately caught fire. I ran to the scene, but could not reach the pilot, he was killed instantly." Mr Chorley wrote a small article on the accident and contacted Nawrocki's wife and daughter being able to tell them the details of his death so long afterwards.

Grave of Sergeant Tadeusz Nawrocki of No. 315 Squadron after crashing in a Spitfire near Lancaster in July 1942. Buried at Our Lady's Church, Formby.
APF

Another Kill

14 AUGUST TURNED out to be quite a day for No 315 Squadron. They had been "Adopted" by Virginia Cherril, the Countess of Jersey and she was their guest of honour on the occasion of the visit by the senior Polish Air Force Officer, Air Marshal Ujejski from the Air Ministry. After a parade at which several members of the Squadron were presented with awards gained whilst in action with No 11 Group, the guests took their places for a display of formation flying. At that moment Green Section, which was at readiness led by Flight Lieutenant Miksa in Spitfire BL751 and Sergeant Pilot Malek in AA929, were scrambled. They took off at 11.20 under Woodvale Sector control and were vectored to a point ten miles north- of Amlwch, Anglesey then North to fifteen miles North-East of Clay Head thence east after a few minutes and orbited at twenty nine thousand feet. Malek saw a Ju88 proceeding towards Barrow-in-Furness at twenty two thousand feet and called up Miksa who was still in orbit to tell him he was giving chase. They dived to twenty two thousand feet, closed in and the enemy gunner opened fire but missed to starboard. At three hundred and fifty yards Malek opened fire from three quarters astern and above giving a burst of one second with cannon and saw strikes on the enemy's port wing between engine and root. With the range closing he gave a final

Polish Guard of Honour in one of the hangars in honour of the Countess of Jersey and AVM Ujejski in August 1942. The station Miles Magister can just be seen to the left. *Group Captain J.A. McDonald*

burst of both cannon and machine gun. He thought his ammunition was exhausted and broke away to port climbing well above the enemy whose rear gunner had now ceased firing.

Malek now noticed oil droplets on his own cockpit cover and white smoke pouring from his spinner, soon the oil was all over his windscreen and he opened the canopy to see the enemy below at about nineteen thousand feet, proceeding in evasive weaves towards Barrow. Realising that he had been hit, he made for Squires Gate where he landed safely. Miksa then attacked giving a few squirts but saw no strikes. He followed the enemy aircraft down to four thousand feet in the direction of the Barrow balloon barrage and as it entered he pulled away, landing safely at Woodvale at 12.40. Unfortunately, no definite results were gained and a damaged aircraft was claimed.

A few weeks earlier No 256 Squadron was on patrol when Flight Sergeant B J Wild and Sergeant R W Gibbons, in a Beaufighter I, made contact with an enemy aircraft five hundred feet below them at night. Contact was lost and no

The Countess of Jersey, Virginia Cherrill being entertained by No. 315 Squadron on 14 August 1942. Squadron Leader Wiorkiewicz seated left, surrounded by Squadron pilots. *Group Captain J.A. McDonald*

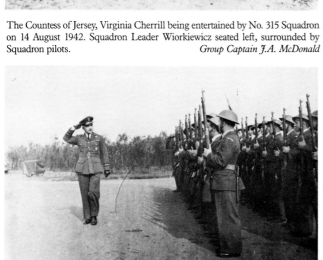

Polish Air Vice Marshall Ujejski reviewing members of No.315 Squadron during his visit with the Countess of Jersey in August 1942.
Group Captain J.A. McDonald

Air Vice Marshall Ujejski decorating Flight Lieutenant Falkowski and his rear gunner in 1942. *Group Captain J.A. McDonald*

Grave of Flying Officer J.J. Sawiak of 315 Squadron. He crashed after attacking a Ju88 and died of injuries in a Dublin hospital.   *APF*

American Red Cross Mobile Canteen toured the sites giving refreshments to the ground crews who had to work in the open in all weather, note the coats. Hot tea and 'wads' must have been very welcome.   *G.A. Peakman*

action took place. No 256 was scrambled ten times in August and three times in September but no enemy contact was made.

No 315 Squadron continued patrols and sent a Section to Valley to enlarge the area it covered and also gave greater convoy protection. The Valley detachment claimed another success for the Squadron on 23 August when Black Section was scrambled at 07.57 comprising Flying Officer Sawiak and Sergeant Lisowski with orders to patrol Bardsey Island. Lisowski ran into sand on take-off and tipped his Spitfire on its nose. Taking off in a second aircraft a few minutes later, Sawiak reported that he was in contact with the enemy at 08.34 but he was not seen by his No 2. After that R/T contact was broken off although the point of contact was given to Lisowski he saw no trace and landed at Ballyhalbert, Northern Ireland, short of fuel, at 09.30. On return to Valley he said that pilots on operations from Ballyhalbert had seen Sawiak break away from combat at about five hundred feet and that as they did not experience return fire from the Ju88 they assumed that he had killed the rear gunner. The Ballyhalbert Section then attacked but did not see Sawiak again and could give no reason why he broke away unless he had been hit. Sawiak crash landed near Dublin and was taken, badly wounded, to hospital where he later died of his injuries. It was later learned that the Ju88 had crash landed in Southern Ireland. Sawiak, who was only twenty three years old, was returned to England and was buried with full military honours at Our Lady's Church, Formby a few days later.

The rest of August was taken up with defensive patrols and training plus co-operation with No 256 Squadron. On 2 September, No 315 were delighted to be informed that they were to move back to Northolt on 5th and spent the last few days packing up and saying farewell to the friends they had made in Southport and Formby. At the last minute it was decided that eleven pilots were not yet sufficiently experienced to return to Northolt and they had to unpack to be left with a few aircraft for exhaustive training for the next eleven days prior to rejoining their Squadron. The Squadron undertook their final patrol on 5 September when they were relieved by No 317 (Polish) Squadron arriving from Northolt.

The third Polish Squadron to be based at Woodvale in succession, No 317 had been visited by the Polish President the day before they departed from Northolt. Led by Squadron Leader S F Skalski to Woodvale the Squadron had suffered terribly at Northolt and Exeter before that. Whilst at Exeter on 15 March the Squadron was returning from operations low on fuel when they lost the airfield in poor visibility resulting in ten aircraft crashing, the CO being killed and three others being injured, only two aircraft landed safely. A month later they were back in business at Northolt and after six months front line action with No 11 Group swopped places with No 315 Squadron for rest and recuperation at Woodvale.

Like No 315, No 317 Squadron was to provide daylight cover for Merseyside and No 9 Group and undertook their first

American Red Cross ladies on the airfield circa February 1943.   *APF*

Cavendish House used as an Officers' Mess until the communal site was completed. Woodvale railway station is to the right with a steam engine visable in the goods yard. Concrete blocks can be seen by the bridge to block it in case of invasion. 1944.

sector recce on 8 September, delayed due to luggage being lost en route. Intensive training continued with several new pilots joining the Squadron. Formation practices, air to air firing, Home Guard co-operation and local flights made up the new routine. The first scramble was on 28 September when Red Section took off at 10.40 and climbed to seventeen thousand feet but did not see the enemy.

No 256 Squadron lost Wing Commander J S Adams DFC on 1 October when he was replaced by Wing Commander T N Hayes DFC. Due to lack of activity at Woodvale the Squadron sent detachments to Valley and Newtownards, Northern Ireland, but there was no action there either and they were withdrawn before the end of October. On 19th the first three Beaufighter Mk VI arrived for the Squadron. Five days later twenty representatives of the Press were shown over the Squadron and aircraft for a public relations exercise.

On 1 October Cavendish House was taken over by the RAF formally and used by officers from the Operations Room who had hitherto been billeted in the Imperial Hotel in Southport. Cavendish House is now demolished. Adjacent to this house was Woodvale Railway Station on the Cheshire Lines linking Liverpool with Southport, Lord Street Station. This station is now part of the ill-fated Winter Gardens scheme lying idle at the time of writing. More and more WAAF personnel had arrived with the result that they had to take over No 1 RAF Site and re-number it No 3 WAAF Site. The AOC-in-C Fighter Command Sir Sholto Douglas KCB, MC, DFC, visited the station for an inspection on 3 October and during his visit he presented the CO of No 317 Squadron, Squadron Leader S F Skalski with a Bar to his DFC. The AOC-in-C was preceded by the AOC No 9 Group Air Commodore Dickson on 9 September and the new AOC-in-C of Fighter Command, Air Marshall Sir T L Leigh-Mallory CB, DSO visited on 4 January, with fog and snow to welcome him.

During October 1942 Group Captain McDonald was posted to RAF Middle Wallop and his post as station and sector commander was filled by Group Captain V S Bowling. Throughout October 1942, No 317 Squadron was scrambled several times but the enemy did not venture this far North very often no interceptions resulted. The last day of October saw a tragic accident when Squadron Leader R de W K Winlaw and his navigator Pilot Officer C T Ashton of No 256 Squadron were killed when their Beaufighter (X7845) was involved in a mid-air collision with a Wellington bomber over Bangor, North Wales, crashing two miles from the town. No 256 Squadron was taking part in a "Bullseye" exercise and both crews perished in the collision. The Board of Inquiry commenced the following day. Squadron Leader Winlaw was cremated and his ashes scattered over the sea on 8 November which almost saw another accident. Another Squadron pilot, Pilot Officer P Harrison-Yates lost an engine whilst about fifty miles out over the sea but he managed to make Woodvale and land safely. The Squadron lost two further crew members on 7 November when Flying Officer W T E Waller, pilot and Sergeant A E Bushy, observer, died when their Beaufighter crashed near Wellesbourne, Warwickshire, after total instrument failure.

Woodvale's MT Section in 1942.

G.A. Peakman

Settling Down To A Routine

TOWARDS THE end of November, due to poor weather at Woodvale, an air firing party from No 256 Squadron left for a four day exercise at Valley accompanied by four aircraft from No 317 Squadron. Later another detachment left for Ballyhalbert, Northern Ireland, for co-operation with No 153 Squadron and No 317 flew intensive army co-operation patrols from Woodvale. No 256 Squadron had one flight on readiness throughout November and December being scrambled five times but again without result. No 256 was joined by a detachment of No 41 Squadron from Llanbedr, North Wales, on the night of 28/29 November when the CO, Squadron Leader T F Neil DFC and bar led six Spitfires from their base for night interception duties. The sortie is graphically illustrated in Ian Allan's book by Wing Commander T F Neil DFC and Bar, AFC, AE, entitled "From The Cockpit - Spitfire". With the Wing Commander's kind permission I extract some of his recollections:

"Having arrived at Woodvale in the afternoon, we learned that we were to become involved in a 'fighter night', an arrangement in which fighters were sent off and layered at 1,000 ft intervals in the area of a possible target and the likely height of the bombers.

It was some time after 10pm, very dark and the weather indifferent. There are enemy aircraft to the south of us, but apparently no one knows precisely for which target they are heading. After a routine but comprehensive briefing, it is decided that we should position ourselves − just in case. The first to go, I sign the authorization book for my own flight and authorise those for the other five pilots. I then scan the Form 700 of EB-V, my personal aircraft and the one in which I had the engine problem three months earlier and which is fitted with a new Merlin. I note that the engine has completed 46 hrs − nicely run in − although the airframe is much older − 170 hrs. No major difficulties though during the last few flights, everything signed for and correct, my flight from Llanbedr the same afternoon constituting the statutory night-flying test.

Out then into the darkness, Blackness everywhere, a raw damp wind and unseen cloud. In the near distance, a small nodding torchbeam, carefully shielded in the blackout − my crew, guiding me. After getting in and strapping up I wiggle in my seat, anxious to manoeuvre the steel bottle of the dingy away from the bones of my backside, and nod to my fitter who lifts the lolling flap to my cockpit and clips it into place. After which, with a farewell touch to my shoulder, he steps down into the darkness and ducks under the wing to take charge of the chocks which block the two wheels of my Spit. I'm safely in and tied down! Now for it!

Start-up, the engine settles to as steady 1,200 revs. I run up gently to 0lb boost, watching the temperatures and pressures, exercise the Rotol airscrew, mag switches and close the throttle. Pre-taxi checks complete I wave away the chocks, move slowly to the perimeter track and begin to jink − insofar as the narrow concrete strip will allow − Spits being brutes to taxi, the nose stretching so far out in front. Can't make too much of a meal getting to the end of the runway as the engine heats up very quickly and I can't afford to let the temperature get beyond 100 degrees or the engine will boil during take off, spout steam and corruption all over the place and frighten me to death. The main runway approaches, green light from the tower, line up, pre take off checks made and we are rolling nicely down the centre-line, the runway lights falling away downwards astern. In front and all around, nothing but endless blackness, the exhausts of the engine cherry red with snarling effort, everything tight and vibrating.

Up wheels! I change hands on the control column and move the lever to the left, then open up and into the notch. The single green light disappears, the rotating wheels shaking violently until I stop them with a touch of brake. 150 on the clock and climb away. The altimeter registers five hundred feet with the needle moving quickly around the dial.

Neil: Hello Inkpen. This is Mitor 14. Airborne and climbing to patrol line. Any trade?

Sector: Mitor 14. This is Inkpen. Nothing at the moment. Call when in position.

It takes me about 20 minutes to climb to 24,000 ft and having arrived there I throttle back to 0lb boost and reduce the revs to 2,000 − no point in wasting fuel. The ASI shows a little under 200 mph, although I am aware that I am going much quicker in true airspeed terms - about 270 in fact. I decide to check my position.

Neil: Inkpen, this is Mitor 14. At patrol height now. Where am I precisely?

Sector: Mitor 14, we have you 10 miles south of "X" (the controller gave the codeword for Liverpool). Flash your weapon.

Members of Supply Flight outside the station stores in 1943.   *APF*

Stores staff outside the station stores in 1943. Centre: Flight Lieutenant Rivlin.
          APF

Control tower and fire/crash section in 1943. The left side of the fire station is the original barn belonging to New Bronk Farm. As usual at Woodvale the windsock is almost horizontal, but a north west wind is unusual.

I fish around to my right in the dark cockpit and locate the switch which operates my IFF. After which:

Sector: Mitor 14, your position confirmed as 10 miles south of "X"

Neil: Any trade?

Sector: Not a sausage.

Controllers like to appear human now and then!

Having "un-flashed" my weapon, I settle down to the mind-boggling boredom of flying in wide figures-of-eight at 24,000 feet. I reduce my cockpit lights to zero so that I fly entirely on the luminosity of my dials, switch on the gun sight, dimming the fiery granules so that they are barely visible, and turn my gun buttons to "FIRE", just for the hell of it. Thirty minutes pass, then 45, then 50, round and round, back and forth, oh! for a German or two!

After seeing searchlights and asking control if there is any trade they advise:

"Mitor 14. One bogey now twenty/two zero miles south of you, confirmed at angels one-five. Maintain your present height and position".

The crash section in June 1985 showing the stair access to the original hay loft in the barn to New Bronk Farm and the war-time extension. These buildings are due to be demolished in 1991.   *APF*

Ground crew of No. 285 Squadron Defiant. The rear turret has been removed and converted into the control position for the target drogue or small scale aircraft target.   *John Hudson*

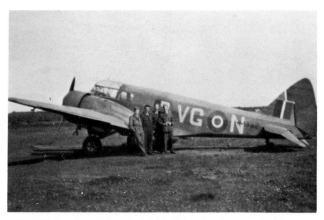

A No. 285 Squadron Oxford used for anti-aircraft and radar calibration work. Woodvale 1942-3.   *John Hudson*

The operation room of the Woodvale Sector which controlled aircraft after Wing Commander T.F. Neil's Spitfire on its night sortie. Photo taken in November 1966 with the building very derelict.   *APF*

A flash of irritation. So What! – do they or don't they want me to intercept? If they do what am I doing waltzing around at 24,000 ft? The searchlights concentrate in a cone, I dive to investigate regardless of Sectors instructions but on reaching 17,000 feet – nothing – a wall of blackness. My pulse returns to normal as reaction sets in. Inkpen and I compare notes, I flash my weapon and am located six miles south of Y – the code word for Llandudno. I have been airborne 72 minutes, apparently, and am advised to return to base without delay. Faintly indignant I ask what has become of the bogey, but no one seems to know.

I head back, on my way to Woodvale I begin to lose height gradually, watching the various instruments on my dashboard reading my descent. After five minutes I am given another vector, zero-seven-eight. I change direction slightly and note that I am at 10,000 feet and descending rapidly with 280 on the clock. Now 4,000 feet; no mountains around here but I mustn't overshoot and drift into the lower hills of the Pennines. I throttle back further to -4lb boost and allow the speed to fall. Soon my ASI is showing 240 and I am down to 2,000 feet.

I am thinking about another vector from control when I happen to see the faint line of the flare-path at Woodvale. Spot on! I circle the airfield at a comfortable distance then join the circuit, switching on my nav lights, something I would not dream of doing had the enemy been close at hand. Down with the wheels - I move the undercarriage level precisely, forward a fraction then down with a slow but deliberate movement so that it slots into its bottom notch. The aircraft gives the briefest of shimmies as the wheels fall away. Curving in now on finals – I push the airscrew into fully fine and hear the engine note rise as the propeller bites. The line of glim-lamps stretching away obliquely to my left, flattens out. Flaps! All or nothing in a Spit, down they go. Holding off just above the runway, the first flare and floodlight flash past on my left, my nose rising steeply. UP! UP! Small lights stream past. The first touch, the Spit balloons minutely before touching down again and moving waywards to one side. I correct - vigorously! Straight! I kick hard to stop the nose from wandering, eventually stopping, taxiing back, watch the radiator don't let it boil. I follow a torch, stop, the chocks are placed behind the wheels and run the engine gently to get everything circulating. Then the slow-running cut out, the noise dies away and the airscrew clanks to a standstill. After which there is only darkness. And silence broken only by the tick-tick-tick of the exhaust stubs as they begin to cool."

All that was November 1942 – Spitfire from Woodvale and Woodvale Sector Control, then at Aughton Springs, Halsall, in perfect harmony protecting the skies over Merseyside.

The Build Up Continues – Five Squadrons

ON 29 OCTOBER 1942 the Headquarters of No 285 Squadron had moved from Wrexham to Honiley maintaining a detachment at Wrexham. the Woodvale detachment now had two Oxfords and six Defiants, including one target-tug. At the end of January 1943 the Wrexham detachment moved to High Ercall in Shropshire, but the Woodvale detachment continued co-operation with the Army gun batteries, increasing its Oxfords to seven by April and detaching two to Atcham, also in Shropshire, to extend its range of operations.

The four units already operating at Woodvale were joined by a detachment of No 116 (Calibration) Squadron on 10 November 1942 when "C" Flight arrived under the command of Warrant Officer R A Boswell with two Oxford aircraft. This Squadron had its Headquarters at Heston under Wing Commander E D Crundall and was responsible for calibrating and re-calibrating searchlights. The Flight had been at RAF Speke and the two pilots and two air gunners arrived by air, the remaining twenty one members of the ground crew travelling by road. The Squadron was split into four Groups and four Flights (A-D). The Headquarters moved to Croydon on 4 December 1942 and the Flights were A at Croydon, Surrey; B at Weston-super-Mare, Somerset; C at Honiley in Warwickshire and Woodvale; and D at Collyweston, Northants and Church Fenton, Yorkshire. The Squadron undertook responsibility for all calibration for the whole of Anti-Aircraft Command and held sixty aircraft with centralised servicing at Croydon. The few movements carried out had little effect on Woodvale and the small dispersal was sufficient for their purposes. The only recorded accident was a small incident when Sergeant S F Hetherington suffered an undercarriage collapse in Oxford R5974 on 6 June 1943 whilst taxiing over some rough ground. The size of the detachment varied a little with five Oxfords by November 1943, reduced to two again by January 1944. The last co-operation by the Flight was undertaken on 3 September 1944 by Warrant Officer Hetherington and the Flight left for RAF DIgby, Lincs.

Christmas 1943 was the first proper one to be held at Woodvale and was celebrated in the traditional manner with the officers serving lunch to the airmen and senior NCOs. Community singing followed enjoyed by all and in the evening there was a three hour concert party. No 317 Squadron maintained a section at readiness throughout the day until 16.00 when they were stood down. Thus ended the first year of RAF Woodvale. Probably more was achieved in the one year than in any one single year since. It had risen from a muddy field to an active fighter station supporting five units and having an establishment of well over one thousand personnel.

January 1943 started off with a visit on 4th by the AOC-IN-C Fighter Command, Air Marshal Sir T L Leigh Mallory CB, DSO who inspected the station and squadrons and had lunch in the Officers' Mess before departing. Pilot Officer Harrison-Yates boosted the Squadrons' morale on 21 January when he was bounced by a Mosquito of No 456 Squadron which attempted to beat him up in his comparatively outdated Beaufighter. Harrison-Yates applied air brakes, thirty degrees of flap and at one hundred and thirty miles per hour executed a rate four turn and found himself on the Mosquito's tail. He shot his camera gun and effectively "Killed" the Mosquito. On landing the film was posted to No 456 Squadron with 256's compliments! As if an omen, the Squadron received the news the very next day that they were to re-equip with Mosquitos.

The Operations Room was at last completed on 12 January and the temporary room at Aughton Springs, Halsall, closed. Squadron Leader Bain was posted in from RAF Atcham to take over the Room and at last the Woodvale sector was complete. One week later a deputation from the Air Ministry arrived to discuss the possible lengthening of the runways. A scheme was put forward by the Station Commander (unfortunately not detailed in the ORB) and very favourably received by the Air Commodore presiding. An alternative scheme was also suggested and it was decided that both would be surveyed and costed prior to a formal report. At least one of the schemes proposed would have resulted in the diversion on the main road (A565) and it is assumed that the cost prevented this from being undertaken.

On 29 January 1943 the Commanding Officer of No 256 Squadron flew a Mosquito to ensure that the runways were

Warrant Officer Joe Hedge and Flight Sergeant Reg Knight of No. 285 Squadron detachment by one of their Oxford 1 aircraft.   *John Hudson*

Senior NCO's of No. 256 Squadron line up in front of one of their new Mosquitoes, 1943.

G.A. Peakman

long enough for regular operations by Mosquitoes and fortunately concluded that they were. Several more patrols were flown in Beaufighters in January without result and by the beginning of February the Squadron had still not received its new aircraft. No 317 Squadron continued training and one Flight was ordered to prepare for a detachment to Northolt for practice Rhubarbs on 12th. However this was cancelled at short notice. On 15 January the Squadron managed forty two sorties and continued night flying until 21.45. Many scrambles were ordered but the only firing was for a flight at a time on four day detachments to RAF valley and the only excitement occurred when Flying Officer Birtus overturned whilst taxiing after a training flight due to lack of brake pressure; he was not hurt but his Spitfire Vb was badly damaged. The Squadron received a signal ordering it to Kirton-in-Lindsey, Lincs, on 10 February and feverish activity resulted as they packed. The last two sorties from Woodvale were completed on 9th and the Flight recalled from Valley. All seventeen aircraft were ready for the AOC of No 9 Group, Air Vice Marshal Whitworth, arrived to see them off on the morning of 10th only to find them grounded due to bad weather. After three frustrating days they finally left on 13th joining the ground crews who had prepared their new station for them. Flight time to Kirton was 65 minutes.

The bad weather was responsible for the loss of a crew from No 256 Squadron on 9 February when Flight Lieutenant D Toone and Pilot Officer W F Hutchings were reported missing twenty miles north west of Squires Gate on Ground Controlled Interception (GCI) exercise. Sergeant Jenkins was acting as a target when Toone's aircraft was seen to disappear and was never seen again. The wreckage was not recovered and the search called off two days later, Sgt Jenkins returned safely.

First Typhoons

NO 195 SQUADRON had formed at RAF Duxford, Cambs, on 18 November 1942 receiving its first Typhoon Ib eleven days later. After having first moved to Hutton Cranswick, Yorks, it arrived at Woodvale to replace No 317 Squadron on 13 February after being held up by the weather, which delayed No 317's departure' and some aircraft were diverted to Church Fenton, Yorks. The Squadron was still training up on type and had a few Hurricanes for pilot training. The officers were billeted in a house called "Woodhey" near the airfield and they settled down to some hectic and traumatic training on this new type. Squadron Leader D M Taylor had several problems including the new aircraft, sand and a new squadron to shape up. The first incident occurred on 18 February when Sergeant Lindsay crashed wrecking his Typhoon close to the airfield. Fortunately he got clear without injures. Engine problems with the Sabre II engine were to plague the Squadron for some time. Morale improved on 20th when a Lockheed P-38 Lightning was brought in by the USAAF for mock attacks and performance matching with the Typhoon successfully outmanoeuvring the American aircraft. By the end of February 1943 the Squadron had fifteen Typhoons (Mk IA & IBs) two Hurricanes and a Tiger Moth.

Air firing commenced as a Squadron on 1 March and the unit was able to man a readiness section on 8th with another section on thirty minutes standby. The same day saw the first scramble but no contact with the enemy. No 256 was now slowly converting onto Mosquitoes and the pilots were slowly passing through the Fighter Interception Unit at RAF Ford, Sussex, although the first Mosquitoes were not received at Woodvale until 15 April. Pilot Officer Harrison-Yates lost his life on 10 March in a Beaufighter when flying on a patrol with his navigator, Sergeant W Patterson. He lost an engine and after skilfully bringing a crippled aircraft back once before, failed to make the runway and crashed onto the station playing field, Beaufighters being very difficult to handle on one engine.

256 Squadron Mosquito being alligned for gun tests with gun butts at Woodvale.
G.A. Peakman

Sergeant Patterson had only slight injuries and shock but Harrison-Yates died of his injuries. The funeral service was held the next day and his ashes were scattered over the Irish Sea by one of the Squadron's aircraft.

Although the first Mosquito arrived for No 256 Squadron on 15 April, the unit was ordered to move to RAF Ford on 25 April, a special train leaving Woodvale station (Cheshire Lines Railway – see location plan) at 09.30 in the morning and arrived at Ford at 20.00. The air party left at noon and the Squadron was on readiness at Ford on the first night of it's arrival. The unit's first kill occurred on 8 May when a Dornier Do 217 was shot down by Flying Officer J A Green and Sergeant A E Waiting, thirty miles off Worthing. After only four months at Ford the Squadron returned to Woodvale with its new Mosquitoes on 25 August ready to train up prior to moving to Malta.

On 5 March the RAF Andreas, Isle of Man, Operations Room closed and Woodvale took over it's operational responsibility absorbing it's sector as from 05.45. Little enemy activity was seen but the air sea rescue duties of No 275 Squadron, flying Anson and Walrus aircraft, were controlled

256 Squadron with Wing Commander T.N. Haynes DFC (with dog) in centre, in front of a squadron Mosquito in the summer of 1943.
G.A. Peakman

Squadron Mosquito on a bright sunny day at Woodvale in 1943. *G.A. Peakman*

from the Woodvale Operations Room. No 275 was in constant demand for aircraft lost in the Irish Sea and the co-ordinated search was now controlled from Woodvale.

No 195 Squadron was still having problems with sand and unreliable engines. Sergeant Jones crashed Typhoon DN474 on 9 March writing it off and putting himself on the danger list for several days. Flying activity took the form of formation flying, air to air firing, practice Rhubarbs, target towing (Hurricane), Sector recces, GCIs, dog fighting, sector attacks, cine gun practice, calibration, battle climbs and low flying. A scramble on 3 April took two aircraft to Anglesey with one crash landing at Mona with engine failure, badly damaging the aircraft. On 9 April the unit suffered another fatality when Sergeant Walter A Dixon, a Canadian pilot, crashed in DN424. He was with A Flight and Squadron member Ken Sharples remembers the incident writing:

Sergeant W.A. Dixon's headstone at St Peter's Church, Green Lane, Formby.
APF

"The above pilot was with A Flight and on take off in a Typhoon did not gain sufficient height at the end of the runway and caught the telegraph wires by the railway and crashed immediately after the railway lines on what I believe is a golf course. The railway line would be the Freshfield – Southport line.

Sgt Dixon was killed immediately, the aircraft did not catch fire. I myself was in B Flight, the nearest Flight to the end of the runway and the crash. I ran (with others) to give assistance but the fire tender arrived before us and we were ordered back to the Flight. I was a member of the funeral firing party. Sergeant Dixon was buried at St Peter's Church, Green Lane, Freshfield.

This incident was put down to pilot error but the Typhoons suffered from sand being ingested into the air intake and special mild steel covers were manufactured for the Woodvale Squadron to prevent this. They were painted with black and yellow stripes to ensure they were removed before flight and painted with the individual aircraft number by the fitters to ensure that no-one purloined his! The Squadron was in two flights, "A" and "B" "A" operated from the new buildings and dispersals on the south end of the airfield whilst "B" Flight operated out of the old Railwayside Farm house mid way along the railway but also operating out of blast protected dispersals. During April No 195 Squadron was only scrambled twice and again without result. The Commanding Officer went on a Fighter Leaders course at RAF Charmy Down, Wilts and came back with many new ideas for the unit to practice. On 16th another aircraft was almost lost when Pilot Officer Morgan crash-landed at Warton landing just short of the runway on the mud bank; fortunately he was not injured and the aircraft was salvaged.

Ken Sharples continues:

"A Flight had a wooden hut on the airfield for their crew room and we in "B" Flight had the farm house. Inside the farm house was a black painted square where the Squadron ground crews had their names chalked up to show what aircraft they were on. We had two petrol bowsers, one pulled by a Fordson tractor and the other by a David Brown tractor.

There were blast bays for the aircraft and there was also a low corrugated iron hangar (all adjacent to "B" Flight) I can't remember much use being made of the hangar, it was too open.

Our billets were adjacent to a lane where the huts had imitation doors painted on their sides and when airmen came back from Southport a little drunk they could not find the

A similar photo is seen earlier of the American Red Cross Club Mobile Canteen feeding some of the Woodvale ground crew at one of the dispersal flight offices in 1944.
APF

Woodvale Sector Ops Room in June 1988 looking south east.   *E.F. Cheesman*

right door to get into the hut. I only remember Woodvale having these false doors.

The Salvation Army used to serve tea and "wads" on the clear ground across the road from the guard room. The Scarisbrick Hotel was one of the meeting places for a pilots night out.

A lady taxi driver used to meet the train at Freshfield Station and run airmen back to a road near the camp. I myself did not use this service more than a couple of times as it was too dear for an AC2 Flt/Mech/Eng (as I was at that time). I think my pay was just over 3/- (15p) a day then. I used to walk back to camp!"

On 3 May 1944 the Squadron learned that due to severe difficulties with the Napier Sabre engines powering the Typhoons, there would be no more new engines from the manufacturers for seven weeks. The two flights were amalgamated during the emergency and used each others' aircraft flying on alternate days. Fortunately the sector was now very quiet and they were able to provide the necessary crews for

readiness sections. A scramble on 11th turned out to be a lost Hudson returning from Gibraltar and at very short notice the Squadron was ordered to move to Ludham on 13th, the first aircraft leaving after ninety minutes notice. The main party left on 14 May but eight aircraft were left at Woodvale without engines. The ORB stated that Ludham was very operational after Woodvale and the first kill was achieved by Sergeant R A Hough only the next day when he shot down a Me109 over Southwold. The Squadron's Tiger Moth left on 14th with three Typhoons and the Hurricane on 17th, the four remaining as soon as engines became available.

No 285 Squadron was operating approximately nine sorties a day out of Woodvale. On 7 May 1943 Sergeant Duckworth was returning from co-operation with heavy AA and was approaching to land in Oxford X7280 when he suddenly flew inland, lost height and crashed after hitting an anti-landing post. The aircraft was wrecked and he died of extensive injuries after battling for life for five months. In July the first Martinet arrived and the detachment now had seven Oxfords, two Defiants and the Martinet. On 10 July a B-24 Liberator of the USAAF en route to the UK from Gander, Newfoundland became lost in severe weather. It was contacted by the Woodvale Sector Control and vectored to Woodvale. A Beaufighter attempted to guide the aircraft in but failed and Flight Sergeant Bolland of No 285 Squadron volunteered to go up in an Oxford and guide it in. Permission was at first refused due to the severe bad visibility but this was subsequently given and he successfully brought it in to a safe landing aided by an imposing display of pyrotechnics from flying control. Flight Sergeant Bolland was immediately awarded a green endorsement for his skill. A few days earlier Sergeant Burgess of the same Squadron flew his Defiant into a flock of pigeons whilst over Heysham on AA co-operation. One of the birds penetrated the canopy hitting him in the face inflicting multiple cuts. Fortunately he was able to land safely at Squires Gate. The day after the Liberator incident the weather was still bad and two Beaufighters from No 406 Squadron were diverted in to Woodvale.

The Station Sick Quarters site still exists in 1991 albeit used as a farmers storage and barn facility. Photographed in March 1991 they are remarkably intact. *APF*

Except for the Station Sick Quarters – the only other remaining dispersed buildings comprise the WAAF Mess on the WAAF Communal Site seen here in March 1991.   *APF*

Constant Moving of Squadrons

DURING EARLY August No 63 Operation Training Unit commenced forming at RAF Honiley, Warwicks, (HQ No 285 Squadron) and the possibility of the Headquarters and Maintenance Flight of No 285 moving to Woodvale was discussed. It was agreed that space was available and the HQ and Maintenance Flight moved on 27 August. Flight Sergeant Bolland was to have an eventful few days, after receiving his green endorsement he had just taken off in Martinet MS507 when the engine cut and he had to make a forced landing at Harrington Barracks at Freshfield. He hit a barrack hut in the landing and the aircraft burst into flames being full of petrol. Fortunately he was pulled from the wreckage by two soldiers and was almost unhurt.

The dispersals previously occupied by Nos 195 and 256 Squadrons were not left empty for long as No 198 Squadron arrived from Manston and Martlesham Heath (Detachment) on 15 May with Squadron Leader J Manek as Commanding Officer. The Squadron had reformed as a fighter/ground attack unit, originally with Hurricanes and recently converted to Typhoon Mk IA and IB, keeping one Hurricane and a Tiger Moth by the time of the move to Woodvale. The Squadron's fifteen aircraft took part in a "Ramrod" on Andreas on 20th and the AOC arrived two days later to discuss the possibility of the Squadron taking over a bombing role and the effect it would have on their training. However, it continued to provide daylight cover to the Merseyside area; Red Section scrambling on 19 May and again on 26th ordered to patrol Lancaster at ten thousand feet. Ten tenths cloud prevailed to the north of base up to nine thousand feet. At this height Pilot Officer Walters waggled his wings and broke away. He was next seen by the Royal Observer Corps at St Annes and hit the sea about one mile offshore. The other pilot, Pilot Officer Williams abandoned due to adverse weather conditions and also nearly hit the ground with cloud down to five hundred feet. The Commanding Officer took off immediately to look for Walters but only found a pool of oil. The aircraft was uncovered at low tide the following day but Walters' body was not recovered until 5 June. After a funeral ceremony at Squires Gate Pilot Officer Robert Ralph Walters was buried at St Annes.

The Squadron was made up of aircrew members from Canada, Australia and Britain with a Czech Commanding Officer. It worked up at Woodvale but was soon to move, first with a rumour that it would go to Ayr in Scotland. At last news was received on 4 June that they were to move the next day to Martlesham Heath, Suffolk, to the joy of all members. The unit left for Martlesham on 5th and, for a change, were not hampered by bad weather. At its new home its first operation comprised covering USAAF Boeing B-17s on their return from daylight bombing raids on Europe. No 198's dispersal lay empty for seven days until No 322 (Dutch) Squadron arrived from Westhampnett, a satellite of RAF Tangmere in Sussex.

No 167 (Gold Coast) Squadron disbanded at Westhampnett and on arrival at Woodvale reformed as No 322 Squadron. The personnel remained the same under the command of Squadron Leader A C Stewart who was re-posted to command. All the remaining personnel of No 167 Squadron were also re-posted en bloc to No 322. The Squadron's pilots flew in, taking over readiness which had been held temporarily by No 501 Squadron for one week, and was on permanent readiness by 15 June. The Squadron was to slowly become wholly Dutch manned and train up at Woodvale, the first batch of Dutch pilots arrived on 16 June. A few scrambles kept the readiness section on its toes during June and July and the ORB notes that the British and Dutch got on well together. On 16 July six of the Squadron's Spitfire Vbs left for Llanbedr, near Harlech, for temporary cover against enemy reconnaissance flights but were recalled a week later after no sightings. Two Beaufighters were vectored into Woodvale for an emergency landing in bad weather on 11 July and a Mosquito from Digby was given an emergency homing and landed safely on 13th. No 322 Squadron members bought a parrot on 27 July but it was noted that it could not yet talk. It was adopted as the Squadron's mascot but recorded that it undertook a sector recce alone on 21 August when some-one let it out of its cage. It flew around for a while and did a good landing prior to returning to

The remains of a dispersal by the Liverpool/Southport railway in January 1973 showing a barn belonging to Railwayside Farm which was used by the ground crews. The flat roofed building was a night crew sleeping billet with triple rows of bunks inside. *APF*

Remains of dispersal flight offices and stores in 1973 awaiting demolition after over twenty years of disuse. The last occupiers being No. 186 Gliding School. *APF*

The W/T towers were originally located behind St Peter's School, Freshfield, off Deansgate Lane North being replaced by a new tower on the airfield in the mid 1970's *APF*

its hangar! Three days later the Squadron moved dispersal to make room for the returning No 256 Squadron from Ford. The following day one of the Squadron's aircraft belly landed and overturned, not injuring the pilot. The aircraft was being turned back onto its wheels when it fell on the station engineering officer bending under its tail badly injuring his back.

Captain K C Kuhlmann, DFC (SAAF) arrived to take over the Squadron from Squadron Leader Stewart on 31 August, just in time to celebrate Queen Wilhelmina's birthday which was done in traditional Dutch style with beer and salted herrings being the only items on the menu. A few days later Blue Section had been scrambled to intercept an X raid (unidentified aircraft) near Dublin, but did not find the enemy.

The Woodvale Operations Room scrambled No 275 Squadron from Andreas, Isle of Man, many times for air sea rescue duties. On 21 July a Lancaster was missing and an Anson crashed off the Calf of Man being rescued by a launch and taken off by a Walrus of No 275 Squadron. The next day "A" Flight of No 32 Squadron carried out "Rhubarbs" on

Wigtown and on 23rd Nos 306 and 308 Squadrons operated out of Woodvale for practice escort duties with USAAF B-17 Fortress formations.

No 9 Group Communications Flight operating out of Salmesbury, being the closest airfield to Barton Hall, arrived at Woodvale on 5 August under Flight Lieutenant Ryalls as the runways at Salmesbury were being repaired. This Flight operated several types on communications duties including Leopard Moths, Hurricanes, Master III, Oxford, Vega Gull and Mentor (mostly impressed civilian aircraft) and returned to Salmesbury on 26 August. Prince Bernard of the Netherlands visited the Squadron on 7 August arriving in a No 256 Squadron Mosquito flown by Flying Officer Sykes. After visiting No 322 Squadron at dispersal he returned to Northolt. Two days later, on 9 August, a specially equipped Mosquito arrived from Farnborough for IFF tests with RDF at Rhuddlan, North Wales, carrying out tests with the Woodvale Sector the following day and being replaced by a Beaufighter also from Farnborough. Four of No 322's aircraft left for Valley on 11th for Exercise Driver whilst the remainder of the Squadron continued training. Two more scrambles were ordered on 16th and 19th and two more aircraft written off on 20th and 24th without injury. On 26 August Group Captain T B Prickman arrived from RAF Staff College to take over command of the Station and Sector. At the end of August 1943 the station strength was as follows, including all Squadron and detachment personnel:

128	RAF Officers	10 WAAF Officers
138	WO and SNCOs	9 WAAF SNCOs
1,276	Airmen	462 Airwomen
1,542		481

On 25 August fourteen Mosquitoes of No 256 Squadron returned from Ford and two hectic weeks of kitting up and vaccinations commenced. One half of the Squadron proceeded on leave immediately whilst the remainder packed up and put long range tanks on their aircraft.

Two hundred and fifty airmen were issued with Sten guns and fifty six with rifles and the ORB comments that they hope there are no accidents as most of them "do not know the butt from the barrel!" The equipment was shipped to Middlesborough on 3 September to join the small detachment which had already been sent on 2 July. The Squadron was at last ready to leave Woodvale on 10, September and marched to Woodvale station to a special train at 10.00. In spite of the fact that the movement was supposed to be secret a large crowd of wives, sweethearts and acquaintances was ready to bid them farewell. After a terrible and overcrowded journey by rail to Glasgow and sea to Malta, they eventually arrived in late September but were not operational for over two months after leaving Woodvale. The air party left with the Commanding Officer, Wing Commander G R Park, DFC, on 25 September for Portreath and on to Gibraltar and Malta.

Royal Naval and American Visitors

NO 776 SQUADRON was quietly continuing its task and had two incidents in September – one on 23rd when Chesapeake AL919 had engine failure over the Ainsdale range (HMS Queen Charlotte) and landed with its undercarriage up on the grass at the North end of the airfield; and on 30th when Chesapeake AL950 touched the sea with its propeller whilst on a low (very low!) flying exercise. The pilot just managed to gain sufficient height (about three hundred feet) to reach the airfield and again make a wheels up landing about one hundred yards inside the airfield boundary. On 22 September Group Captain C Walter, OBE, assumed command of the station and on 11 September No 322 Squadron put up twelve Spitfires to escort Princess Mary from Yeadon to the Isle of Man, also providing an escort for her return. October saw several more scrambles and on 30th intercepted three B-17 Fortresses lost in bad weather, two being guided to Woodvale whilst the third continued to Burtonwood, near Warrington. No 275 Squadron at Andreas was scrambled virtually every day to search for lost or missing aircraft, two Ansons searching off Barrow for a lost Martlet on 28, without result.

During November and December 1943 many lost aircraft were vectored to Woodvale for safe landings; three P-47 Thunderbolts on 18 October, three Fortresses on 30th, a Fortress on 4 November, two Wellingtons on 7th, a Beaufighter on 17th and a P-38 Lightning on 11 November.

No 322 Squadron was detached to the Armament Practice Camp at Llanbedr for live firing practice on 16 November, returning on 28th. A period of very bad weather, with temperatures showing nine degrees of frost on the ground and twenty in the air prevented flying for periods in December and the lull in operations was used to practice for a Diver exercise to be held on 18th but this was cancelled at the last minute pushing the Squadron morale even lower. The next day, Blue section guided eleven lost B-24 Liberators to Woodvale (quite a sight on the ground) and heard on 21st that they were considered to be fully operational for No 11 Group and would be moving South on 20 December. Initially, they were informed that they would proceed to Hornchurch, Essex, and take over from No 222 Squadron and their aircraft. However, on Christmas Eve the orders changed to move to

Look east in 1943, note camouflaged runways but the buildings stand out easily.

Hawkinge, Kent, instead and to take over the aircraft of No 350 (Belgian) Squadron. The servicing echelon of No 317 (Dutch) Squadron was not to move however. On 20 December the searchlights of the Woodvale sector were withdrawn, so confident were the authorities that night attacks would not reoccur.

Christmas for the third time at Woodvale was a more glorified affair. Besides there being more personnel on the station, a production named "Woodvale Follies" was presented and ran for five nights. Christmas dinner was served to the airmen and airwomen in the messes by the officers and senior NCOs before the opening performance of the revue in the station gymnasium on the Communal Site. A dance was held in the airmens' NAAFI in the evening. As usual readiness was maintained but the only flying was one sortie to wish the Ops Room staff a "Happy Christmas" from No 322 Squadron. An informal party was held in the Officers' Mess on Boxing day and an evening dance in the NAAFI with a further party to wish No 322 farewell on 29th. Full flying programmes were carried out on 27th and 28th and a party was held on the WAAF Site after the final performance of the "Woodvale Follies" on 29th. No 322 Squadron flew to Hawkinge on 30th becoming operational on 4 January 1944 undertaking their first operation over enemy territory escorting bombers over Northern France.

Beaufighter If's were added to the inventory of No 285 Squadron in September 1943 when the first three arrived on 17th. They were flown in from No 51 Maintenance Unit at Lichfield as the response to a need for faster aircraft for searchlight co-operation. Officially they were on temporary issue for six months and brought the establishment of the Squadron up to nine Oxfords, two Defiants, one Martinet and three Beaufighters. Not all the aircraft were at Woodvale as detachments were currently at Honiley, Warwicks, and High Ercall in Shropshire, with one Oxford at Drem in Scotland. With the increase in size of the Squadron it moved offices to the newly vacated Defence Site on the northern boundary of

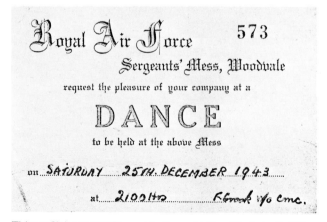

Royal Air Force   573
Sergeants' Mess, Woodvale

request the pleasure of your company at a

DANCE

to be held at the above Mess

on SATURDAY 25TH DECEMBER 1943

at 2100hrs   FBrook i/o cmc.

Ticket to Christmas 1943 Dance at the Sergeants' Mess, Woodvale. *M. Nickson.*

the airfield and utilised the dispersals close by. On 22 November the establishment was again reviewed and increased to eleven Oxfords plus three in reserve; three Beaufighters plus one in reserve and one Tiger Moth with none held in reserve.

Pilot Officer Smith and Flight Sergeant A W Printer in Oxford LX462 on a night flying test undershot the runway and went through the boundary fence damaging the starboard undercarriage, wing and prop but not the crew fortunately. During early December the High Ercall detachment was called in and on the last day of 1943 the Squadron held eight Oxfords, two Beaufighters, one Defiant and a Tiger Moth with detachments at Honiley, Castle Bromwich and Drem. A further detachment was sent to Croydon for one month on 4 January and was moved to West Malling on 9 February. Two days later the Squadron received its first Hurricane when LE508, a Mk IV, flew in from No 22 Maintenance Unit at Silloth. Routine co-operation was maintained during the first

half of 1944 even though most searchlights in the immediate area had been withdrawn. There were very few incidents but changes continued with the closure of the Drem detachment; the moving of the West Malling detachment back to Croydon on 20 February and a temporary detachment at Collyweston from 6th to 20 May.

No 222 (Natal) Squadron held its farewell party at Suttons at Hornchurch (this station's original name was Sutton Farm) on 29 December at the same time as No 322 Squadron at Woodvale. the majority of the Squadron flew its Spitfire LFIX's to Woodvale the following day taking over No 322(s dispersal and arrived just in time for a big New Year's Eve party with a US dance band and many famous musicians. Flying training for 1944 commenced on 2 January and on 6th No 315 (Czech) Squadron landed and spent the night on the station en route from Ibsley, Hants to Ayr, Scotland, held up by bad weather.

Aerial view of Main Site with the recently completed dual carriageway separating the airfield from the dispersal sites where Sick Quarters, Communal Site, Operations Room and six living sites can be seen.

Crown Copyright

First Training Unit

THE WEATHER improved the next day and the first detachment from No 12 (P)AFU arrived from Grantham, Lincs, with sixteen Blenheim Vs, to be known as the "W" Detachment. A conference was held just after Christmas to discuss the possibility of detaching part of the unit to Woodvale whilst new track runways were laid at Grantham. Although Woodvale was very busy, room was found and the advance party arrived on 8 January. No 12 (P)AFU operated almost one hundred aircraft and kept some at Grantham whilst the rest were dispersed to its satellite at Harlaxton. The unit was an advanced training unit for pilots and their crew where they trained as a crew on multi engined aircraft prior to being posted onto their operational types. The pilots would have trained on single engined types on which they would have gained their "wings", moving onto the Advanced Flying Unit (AFU) for conversion onto twin engined aircraft and, maybe, then onto four engined types. On 12th the laying of the Somerfield tracking commenced and the next day Blenheim AZ877 executed a belly landing at Woodvale after the pilot failed to lower his undercarriage. Initially, it was thought that Woodvale may not be suitable and the Senior Training Officer visited Poulton, a satellite of RAF Hawarden built in the grounds of the Duke of Westminster's home at Eaton Hall, near Chester. Here they found insufficient hangar and flight office accommodation but commenced to move the "W" Detachment the following day completing it on 8 February, leaving five aircraft at Woodvale unable to leave as they were awaiting repair. Two additional blister hangars were taken over at Poulton, making three, therefore the proposed use of another airfield at Cranage, was now found unnecessary. Extensive alterations were carried out to the Watch Office at Poulton but the detachment commander was still not happy with the accommodation.

No 9 Group moved its AA School from Speke to Woodvale during January 1944. The object of the school was to give courses to airmen who could then assist station commanders in the training of AA Flights by giving practice in ground to air firing to the airmen detailed to man AA posts. Twin Browning machine guns on Motley stalk mountings were used at Woodvale and heavier guns at HMS Queen Charlotte by arrangement with the Royal Navy. Each course contained nineteen or twenty airmen and three or four courses were held per month. Due to the decreased enemy activity in No 9 Group's area, the courses were discontinued in August 1944.

On 9 March, the Commanding Officer of No 12 (P)AFU flew to Sutton Bridge with the intention of transferring the detachment there but it moved back to Woodvale on 21 March, eight days before Grantham was renamed Spitalgate. The "W" Detachment now settled down with few mishaps except a wheels up landing on 25 June when there was a large influx of aircraft from the parent unit due to Woodvale being the only place with weather suitable for flying. On 6 July Blenheim V BA783 crashed when it overshot after a racing port engine had been stopped and the pilot tried to go round again on one engine. The aircraft cartwheeled into the ground from about one hundred feet, seriously injuring the crew of two who were flown to the RAF Hospital at Cosford.

On 16 August the runways at Spitalgate were complete and the detachment returned to the main unit there leaving Woodvale very much quieter.

No 222 Squadron took part in a civil defence exercise at Bolton on 30 January, acting as targets; a "Ranger" on Jurby on 1 February; a practice "Ramrod" on West Freugh on 7 February and a "Balbo" on 8th. Twelve aircraft took part in the Balbo, then a typical day evolved with a battle formation and tactics. At 10.00 the readiness section broke off leaving ten aircraft to carry on, the Squadron landing at 10.30. As soon as they had refuelled "A" and "B" Flights were back in the air; A Flight on formation practice and B Flight practice flying and cine gun practice. After lunch A Flight undertook a practice Ramrod on Ireland, the flight sweeping inland for twelve miles and able to get in a few bounces. After refuelling again the Flight was up again for cine gun practice and tail chasing in twos. B Flight carried on practice flying with the small number of aircraft at its disposal. When flying had ceased at 17.45 no less than fifty six flying hours had been achieved by the Squadron and the readiness flight remained.

February was notable for the movement of squadrons that took place. On 11 February No 219 Squadron reported on return from overseas; personnel were paid, issued with railway warrants and sent on leave. The same day the pilots of No 222 Squadron left for Acklington with the servicing echelon proceeding on 14th. The advance party of No 316 (Polish) Squadron arrived from Acklington on 14th, the main party following on 16th. No 219 and its servicing echelon reassembled after leave on 26th. Acklington was an Armament Practice Camp where fighter squadrons would shoot live rounds at both air and ground targets on specified ranges with expert guidance of the range and gunnery officers. Usually the stay at APC's was short – two or three weeks – and took place when the squadron had worked up its new pilots or converted onto new types after a rest and was ready to return to the area of heavy fighting forming the end of a period of training.

No 222 Squadron started packing for its move to Acklington on 12th and left for Catterick, Yorkshire, on 14th in preparation for exercise "Eagle" eventually reaching Acklington on 26th. It only stayed at Acklington until 10 March prior to moving to Hornchurch where it undertook its first real "Ramrod" on 13 March in close support of thirty six B-26 Marauders over Northern France.

No 316 Squadron arrived from Acklington on 16 February occupying No 222's dispersal in the usual way of squadron change rounds and immediately became operational providing a readiness section. No 316 Squadron took part in army co-operation exercises on 22 February plus another on 25th. Four pilots of No 322 Squadron landed en route to Ayr unable to proceed due to poor weather and they took the opportunity to see their old base again. They managed to continue their journey the following day. On their return to Hawkinge, they again landed at Woodvale to refuel and were again unable to leave due to the weather, leaving the next day they were replaced by No 349 Squadron going the other way, North to Ayr for the APC and they also were accommodated for the night. On 1 March, Squadron Leader Hann was posted in to take command of No 285 Squadron and on the following day a Halifax from Skipton on Swale, Yorks, landed with one engine unserviceable.

On 11 February 1944, No 219 Squadron disembarked from SS "Strathmore" at the Princes Landing Stage, Liverpool, and marched to Exchange Station. Taking a train to Ainsdale station they marched to Woodvale where they were sent on disembarkation leave until 26 February. The Squadron returned and found a number of new Mosquitoes waiting for them. The following day the pilots were introduced to AI (Airborne Interception) equipment by the Commanding Officer, Wing Commander Boyd, and four navigators made a trip in AI equipped Wellingtons temporarily based at Woodvale. The first serious flying training took place on 1 March with the first AI practice following two days later. As the Squadron was to be a night flying unit and Woodvale was not suitable for them (reason is not stated), the Squadron was advised that it would move to Honiley, Warwicks. The first two aircraft left on 14th, followed by the rest the next day. The Squadron scored its first success on 27th, one day after a further move to Colerne, Wilts, when Squadron Leader Ellis shot down a Junkers Ju88 near Yeovil.

The Gunnery School at Ainsdale Lido, HMS Queen Charlotte, with the original Lido building (still standing) in dead centre with the temporary war-time buildings surrounding it. Guns and predictors are arranged along the shore line. Pontins Holiday Camp is now located in the foreground area.

End Of The Night Fighters

AS NO NIGHT fighter squadron was now permanently established at Woodvale, the day fighter units had to provide cover although it was never needed. On 5 March one section was scrambled for an X raid (unidentified aircraft) which turned out to be friendly, and were again scrambled on 11th and did a practice "Ramrod" on Ireland on 28th. On 8 March, No 341 Squadron, en route to the APC at Ayr, were accommodated for the night and a Skua of No 776 Squadron crashed into the sea off Southport pier without injury to the crew. On 18th Nos 438, 439 and 440 Squadrons landed for refuelling on the move of the wing from Ayr to Hurn, filling the airfield with their Typhoons; Woodvale being an excellent refuelling point mid way and easy to find on the coast.

On the same day a Lockheed P-38 Lightning, piloted by Lt H W Vallee from Base Air Depot No 2 at Warton, just across the Ribble estuary, crashed on the sand dunes west of the airfield, the pilot being killed and the aircraft totally wrecked. Flight Sergeant Kowalski of No 316 Squadron was also killed after an attempted forced landing after developing engine trouble, being buried in Formby on 25th but the location of his grave is not known. Aircraft movements in the area were very heavy with the USAAF at Warton with constant test flying punctuated by delivery and arrival flights; RNAS Burscough a few miles to the east was training Naval aircrew; Speke still had military flights plus the huge Lockheed facility and Rootes Securities assembling Halifaxes and American fighters. Burtonwood, an even larger USAAF base, with hundreds of movements every day, only twenty miles to the south east. Squires Gate was very close to Warton housing a reconnaissance school with Ansons and Bothas; RNAS Inskip was just to the north with more Navy training aircraft, Hooton Park was opposite to Speke across the Mersey acting as a maintenance unit and some delivery and test flying was being carried out on Hesketh Park foreshore at Southport. This part of England may have been away from the active part of the war but it was certainly very busy indeed. Several aircraft were diverted to Woodvale in emergency with a Naval Hurricane on 11 March and three Fireflies from Burscough on 31st.

The first mention of No 316 Squadron re-equipping with Mustangs was made on 13 April and the Squadron converted itself as they arrived. By 23 April sixteen Mk IIIs had arrived and they took part in their first scramble the following day when the readiness section was scrambled at 05.05 but it turned out to be a lost Wellington at eight thousand feet. The next day ten Mustangs were put up in a battle formation. Mustangs were not seen around the Lancashire sky for long however, as they moved to Coltishall, Norfolk, on 28 April with Squadron Leader P Niemiec as Commanding Officer and still retaining at least four Spitfires on strength. From Coltishall the Squadron too part in shipping patrols, convoy escorts and scrambles, not dissimilar to their duties at Woodvale. First action was seen on 2 June when they went to Holland on a "Day Ranger".

The defences of Merseyside were not left unprotected as No 316 Squadron was replaced the day before they left, by No 63 Squadron, on 27th, flying Hurricanes but currently

A P-38 Lightning at Burtonwood after a landing accident in 1945. This is the same type that Lieutenant Vallee crashed in near Woodvale on 18 March 1944.

Denver L. Rice

The Station Armoury on Main Site where all routine servicing, overhauls and repairs and modifications were undertaken. The building had steel bars on all the windows and very high security. After the departure of No. 611 Squadron it lay unoccupied until occupied by 1430 Squadron ATC. It was demolished in 1990 and the new 10AEF building erected on the base. *APF*

converting on to Spitfires. No 63 Squadron moved from Turnhouse, near Edinburgh, and on the morning of 28th were able to mount a dawn to dusk readiness with two Hurricanes on standby and two others at thirty minutes availability. The first scramble was on 30th but this turned out to be a friendly aircraft. The Squadron maintained a detachment at RAF Ballyhalbert, Northern Ireland, and for part of May, another detachment at RAF Dundonald was also manned. The rest of May was spent undertaking practices with Spitfires, air-sea rescue assistance, Army co-operation and interception exercises. The Squadron received a signal to move to Lee-on-Solent on 28th but unfortunately lost one of its Spitfires on 21st. Flying Officer G L Storey spun whilst in a steep turn and crashed into some houses in Ainsdale, just to the north of the airfield. His Spitfire burst into flames and he was killed; two civilians attempting to rescue him were also badly burned. On 25 and 27 May the detachments from Ballyhalbert and Dundonald respectively were withdrawn to Woodvale in preparation for the move and the Commanding Officer, Flight Lieutenant M A Doniger, led his eleven Spitfires to Lee-on-Solent on the morning of 28th, leaving No 9 Group without fighter cover for the first time. However, the Squadron did not stay and returned to Woodvale to continue to provide fighter cover on 3 July having gained nine Spitfires at Lee.

The move to Lee was to fly protective patrols over the Normandy beaches for the D-Day landings as every possible fighter was committed to protect the landings and the Air Ministry considered it safe for the Woodvale Sector to be left without cover for a month. The orders of the day on 6 June (D-Day) from General Eisenhower, the Supreme Allied Commander, were carried to Northern Ireland by Warrant Officer S Craven in a No 285 Squadron Beaufighter. Although the weather was bad, it was flown without mishap. No 285 Squadron now had six Oxford Is, one Beaufighter, two Hurricane IICs and one Tiger Moth. Detachments were now at Honiley, Warwicks; Fairwood Common, South Wales and Colerne, Wilts.

In May a party of WAAF and RAF took part in a parade in Southport as part of the beginning of Salute the Soldier week. RAF equipment was loaned as part of the exhibition being one of the features and personnel gave talks on prop assemblies and dinghies. 28 June saw the fifth anniversary of

the formation of the WAAF and a parade of available airwomen took place, the salute being taken by the Station Commander, followed by a special service by the padre, Rev E A T Attwater. In the evening a very successful dance was held on No 1 WAAF Site. The travelling entertainers of ENSA presented a variety show "All For Fun" on 1 May and "Heather Mixture" on 17 July. A station sports day was held at Ainsdale on 5 July and in the inter section competition, the large numbers of No 12 (P)AFU dominated the list of winners.

During July, No 63 Squadron, under Squadron Leader M Savage, kept a detachment at Ballyhalbert and undertook several practice scrambles, assisted in air sea rescue and prepared for its new role of a tactical reconnaissance squadron. The policy therefore dictated that training was to concentrate on army co-operation but no suitable facilities existed at the station. The previous role of the fighter squadrons at Woodvale was not now so important as no serious enemy attacks had been reported for well over a year. On 4 July two aircraft were scrambled to shoot down a barrage balloon which had broken free and on 14th two were scrambled to attempt to locate a Dakota which had crashed into the sea without race. On 6 July command of RAF Woodvale was taken over by Group Captain C Walter OBE.

Due to the continued run down of operations in the North West, the Operations Room in Broad Lane was closed down from 12.00 on 4 August 1944, and the Sector handed over to RAF Church Fenton, Yorks, No 12 Group, the handover being completed by 17.50. The Woodvale Sector therefore ceased to exist and the station came under the control of No 12 Group. Group Captain Walter had a very short stay as Commanding Officer as he was posted to Headquarters Air Defence Great Britain (ADGB) on 18 August. The station passed to Wing Commander E P Gibbs, DFC for three days, then to Wing Commander J W Rayner for six days before finally passing to Wing Commander C R Strudwick on 24 August. The rank of the Commanding Officer now being reduced as the station had lost its Sector status.

No 63 Squadron sought co-operation from the Mustang OTU, No 41, at RAF Hawarden, North Wales, but endured a rather inactive period and finally moved back to Lee-on-Solent on 30 August after recalling its detachments at Eshott, Peterhead and Ballyhalbert. The Squadron's first combat was spotting for naval bombardment of Le Havre on 5 September.

The Barrack Store on Main Site housed furniture and stores. It is now the small-bore indoor range for No. 611 Squadron ATC but has since been totally reclad externally. *APF*

Last Front Line Fighter Squadron

NO 63 SQUADRON was the last of the war-time fighter squadrons to see service at Woodvale, mainly due to the Sector responsibility being vested in Church Fenton. It was also the last fighter squadron in No 9 Group and from now on the Group relied on Typhoons from No 3 Tactical Exercise Unit and by borrowing aircraft from adjoining Groups. On 4 August 1944, No 9 Group Headquarters closed and its responsibilities were taken over by HQ No 12 Group (Fighter Command). No 776 Squadron was still very active with its headquarters at Speke but operating from Woodvale and losing a target glider off HMS Queen Charlotte on 1 August. No. 285 Squadron was also busy keeping a low profile with its routine commitments. The station saw many visitors, several due to the fact that the Palace Hotel in Birkdale was an American Red Cross Club and Rehabilitation Centre and the Sunnyside Hotel in Southport was the HQ of Base Air Depot Area controlling the USAAF bases at Burtonwood, Warton and Langford Lodge in Northern Ireland. These two units caused many visiting USAAF aircraft to Woodvale. During the week ending 5 August 1944, for example, the following aircraft were logged as visitors: four Anson T1's, one Tiger Moth, one Miles Master, three Martinet TT1's, two UC-78 Brasshats, four B-24 Liberators, two B-17 Flying Fortresses, a Spitfire Vb, a Reliant CI and an A-20 Boston. The "W" detachment left Woodvale for Spitalgate on 17 August and the station had more room than ever before.

No 116 Squadron had also kept a small detachment of two Oxfords at Woodvale and they left on 10 September for RAF Digby, Lincs. Woodvale was now left with No 776 Squadron, No 285 and a detachment of No 650 Squadron which was opened on 18 June 1944 with two Hurricane IVs. This Squadron had its headquarters at Cark and operated another detachment at Netheravon. The Squadron had similar commitments to No 285 Squadron operating in conjunction with the Army. On 18 November the Headquarters moved from Cark to Bodorgan, Anglesey, taking over the Ty Croes range (No 4 Royal Artillery Practice Camp) from No 1606 Flight. The Squadron now operated Martinet Is, Hurricane IVs and Tiger Moth Mk IIs keeping another detachment at Cark.

A Dakota air ambulance landed at 23.30 on 10 August with 24 wounded US infantry privates on board. The aircraft had been flying around the west coast of England for four or five hours unable to land owing to bad weather. The morale of the wounded men (most of which had never flown before) was low and some of them were becoming frightened and anxious as they had little or no food for eight or nine hours. It was decided to admit them for the night at Station Sick Quarters as the nearest US hospital was forty miles away. The twenty four filled all the available accommodation including an empty WAAF ward! The US Red Cross Club at the Palace Hotel, Birkdale was contacted and provided many excellent comforts. A convoy of ambulances from the 168th US Army Hospital at Warrington transferred the patients there the next day.

A far worse disaster occurred on 25 October 1944, when a USAAF B-24 Liberator crashed on approach in bad weather on the North West edge of the airfield, close to the dispersal used by No 285 Squadron. The aircraft came from the 704th Bomb Squadron, 446th Bomb Group and took off from its base at Bungay around mid-morning. The crew and passengers numbered about 20, the passengers also being destined for the Palace Hotel at Birkdale as mentioned above. In marginal weather in the circuit at Woodvale the aircraft dragged a wing on final approach as the pilot tried to line up with the runway at the last moment. The aircraft cartwheeled and blew up finishing on the bank near the Liverpool to Southport electric railway line. Some of the airmen were thrown clear in a dazed and injured condition and in danger of being caught in the blaze. Three LMS platelayers who were working close by ran to the burning wreckage and, despite machine gun bullets bursting in all directions, they succeeded in carrying four of the men to safety. One had his clothing on fire and was rescued in the nick of time. Meantime RAF fire-fighters and the local National Fire Service arrived on the scene and rescued some more. Four airmen were killed outright and three more died later in Station Sick Quarters. The remaining thirteen were transferred to EMS hospital in Southport and later the 157th US Army Hospital in Liverpool. The three patients admitted to Station Sick Quarters were given penicillin and intravenous transfusions plus the usual shock treatment, all regrettably dying. One pilot lost a wrist watch but this was returned to him in hospital after it was found in the wreckage. It still worked and he wore it for several years afterwards!

The exodus from Woodvale continued; on 11 November 1944, No 285 Squadron, which had been resident at Woodvale for two and a half years, received orders from Headquarters No 70 Group that it was to move to RAF Andover, Hants, before 20th with a new commitment to No 6 Anti-Aircraft Group instead of No 4 Anti-Aircraft Group in the North West. It was to take over from No 667 Squadron with its Headquarters at Andover and detachments at Middle Wallop and Farnborough. The Squadron left Woodvale on 19th picking up its Fairwood Common detachment en route. The unit comprised fourteen officers, fifteen airmen aircrew, one hundred and fifty two other ranks, six Oxford Is, two beaufighters, four Hurricane IICs and a Tiger Moth. This time, however, the void was filled immediately as a detachment

A consolidated B-24 Liberator seen here on the ramp at Burtonwood near Warrington in 1945. This is similar to the one that crashed at Woodvale on 25 October 1944.   *APF*

The cast of the Pantomine at Christmas 1944 held on the Communal Site for several consecutive nights.

of No 577 Squadron which moved in on the same day from Sealand, filling No 285 Squadron's dispersal. Sealand was too overcrowded and only had a small airfield which was used by No 24 Elementary Flying Training School flying Tiger Moths and it was considered that Woodvale was a far better home for the unit. The Squadron had a monthly target of four hundred hours co-operation and flew five Hurricanes and two Oxfords. During December the aircraft were moved to another dispersal and all rendered immobile at night and guarded as information had been received at Woodvale that German Prisoners of War were planning an escape. This did not, however, materialise. On 30 November the Intelligence Section at Woodvale closed and on the last day of 1944 Flight Lieutenants K H Holmes and A R Spear arrived to command the detachments of No 650 and 577 Squadrons respectively.

January 1945 saw little of note at Woodvale. The number of RAF aircraft and units had sunk to a very low ebb with a few Hurricanes, Masters and the odd Oxford being the only occupants together with No 776 Squadron. No 577 Squadron commenced co-operation with No 19 Initial Training Camp at Harrington Barracks in Formby, with the Military College of Science at Bury, East Lancashire; off St Annes and also supplementing No 776 Squadron at HMS Queen Charlotte. Meanwhile the duties undertaken by "B" Flight of No 650 Squadron were dwindling; "C" Flight was withdrawn from Cark on 6 June and Woodvale's last co-operation flight by the RAF was flown in a Hurricane on 22 March with the 4th Maritime Co-operation Unit at Southport. the Squadron ultimately disbanded on 26 June 1945. The commitments of the "B" Flight were taken over by the detachment of No 577 Squadron at Woodvale, a No 299 Squadron detachment at West Freugh and No 631 Squadron at Llanbedr.

On 13 February a Mosquito piloted by Flight Lieutenant Smith crashed on making an emergency landing at Woodvale, due to the failure of one engine. The pilot was killed but the observer only sustained a fractured arm. The next day another Mosquito piloted by Squadron Leader Cowper, crashed on landing, again with an engine failure, but fortunately this time there were no injuries. On 4 May Warrant Officer T Price of No 577 Squadron detachment crashed in Hurricane LF652 into the sea off Southport and perished. The tide was coming in and his body was not reached until after high tide at 21.30.

The Navy Arrive

WOODVALE'S RESIDENTS now numbered two, No 577 Squadron detachment and No 776 Squadron detachment. The RAF had no further use for the airfield and it was handed to the Royal Navy for the Fleet Air Arm operations on 2 April 1945 and No 577 Squadron detachment became a lodger unit. On 15 February a party of 450 naval ratings had occupied part of the living sites whilst their ship, HMS Duke of York was being refitted in Liverpool as so much room was available. Whilst the RAF were running down Woodvale, the Fleet Air Arm were still building up HMS Ringtail at RNAS Burscough, a six hundred and fifty acre airfield seven miles due east of Woodvale. Burscough had been commissioned on 1 September 1943 to house both front line and training squadrons of the Fleet Air Arm. It often accepted aircraft from carriers arriving in the Mersey and on this April date accommodated No 1790 Squadron with Fireflies, No 707 Squadron with Swordfish, Barracudas, Ansons and Avengers, No 735 Squadron with Barracudas and Ansons, a Station Flight and was reforming No 737 Squadron with Ansons and Barracudas. The station had also been fitted out as a Deck Landing School base with dummy aircraft carrier markings on its runways together with arrester wires.

Due to the commitments already placed on Burscough and the growth of the War in the Far East, Woodvale was commissioned as a "Tender" (satellite) and became HMS Ringtail II on 7 April 1945. The Headquarters of No 776

A vertical view of HMS Ringtail – RNAS Burscough in October 1943. Navy airfield usually had four runways instead of the usual three.

Squadron at last moved to Woodvale on the same day, having lost all its Chesapeakes, Rocs and Skuas and operating for almost the remainder of its time at Woodvale with Martinets and Seafires. The reasons for the transfer of No 776 (FRU) Squadron and the closing of the naval facility at Speke in favour of Woodvale were first of all its immediate availability; Speke was a civil airfield and not only were the operation of winged targets impracticable but also all flying was often curtailed by prevalence of fog. The Fleet Air Arm was building up for the final push in the Pacific and No 889 Squadron had disbanded in Ceylon on 1 June, reforming on the same day at Woodvale being the second FAA unit there. The unit received six Hellcats by 1 July when the second Squadron, B Flight of No 736 Squadron, FAA arrived from Hal Far (Malta). A fighter affiliation unit, this Squadron was training the 11th Aircraft Carrier Squadron in Gryo Gunsight tactics prior to their sailing to the Far east to join the British Pacific Fleet. They had sailed to Malta in HMS Colossus and returned to Woodvale flying Seafires, Beaufighters and a Dominie. The unit operated from Woodvale with a short move to Fearn in Scotland before returning and disbanding here in September 1945.

No 816 Squadron FAA, moved in from Machrihanish, Scotland, and re-equipped with twelve Firefly FR.Is. Once worked up this Squadron moved to Inskip on the Flyde peninsula, on 11 August making room for No 822 Squadron, which moved from Belfast to re-arm with Firefly's. The atomic bombs on Japan heralded the premature end of the war and the immediate effect was the commencement of disbandment of squadrons in both the FAA and the RAF. Woodvale was immediately with No 889 Squadron, (which had a short embarkation on HMS Ravager and at Belfast during August), embarking on HMS Trouncer on 10 September only to disband the following day; followed on 26 September by No 736B Squadron disbanding. No 822 Squadron moved to Burscough, disbanding on 19 February 1946.

The Fleet Requirement Units were dramatically reduced by the Fleet Air Arm and No 776 Squadron was axed in November 1945, most of the aircraft already having been redeployed. Woodvale was left empty for the first time since it opened in 1941. However, the Royal Navy retained control and some limited use of the living accommodation until 28 January 1946 when it was officially de-commissioned and handed back to the RAF.

In the meantime No 577 Squadron had spent some time in the company of the Navy and moved from No 4 to No 1 dispersal on 2 July to make room for No 816 Squadron's Fireflies. During July its last Hurricanes were ferried out and replaced with Vengeances, the first arriving on 7th. The first towing sortie with Vengeance TTs was on 14th and simultaneously the Spitfire Vbs were replaced with Mk XVIs. The Vengeances experienced several engine problems, this two hundred and seventy five mile per hour converted torpedo bomber being grounded in August pending investigations into its fuel tanks, being airborne again by the end of the month.

The Squadron transferred from No 70 Group into the control of No 12 Group (Fighter Command) on 10 July and was warned on 27 September that Woodvale was shortly to close and the detachment was to move. Packing commenced on 3 October and the unit moved to Barrow on 11th leaving one unserviceable Vengeance at Woodvale which finally moved to Barrow on 17th. This aircraft being the last one to fly from Woodvale until the airfield was re-opened for the formation of No 611 Squadron in 1946. With the rundown of all units the end of the war passed quietly at Woodvale with little celebration by the few personnel remaining but there were parties in the messes and a general stand-down for the day.

No 772 Squadron was the last to leave Burscough, on 3 May 1946, and that station was reduced to care and maintenance. After the rear party had removed all valuable and useful equipment, Burscough was handed over to RNAS Stretton, located a few miles to the South East of Warrington, which used the airfield as a sub storage unit for several years, known as the Naval Engine Holding Unit. No further service flying ever took place from Burscough although the remains of the runways and many hangars still remain in 1991.

Vertical view of Woodvale and Freshfield taken on 10 August 1945. Note markings on the end of the runways presumably dummy deck marking for the FAA aircraft. By this time all but two of the blister hangars had gone and the outline of the golf course can be seen immediately south of the airfield with the Old Club House by the railway. A large number of aircraft can be seen parked on the grass between the main runway and perimeter track by the railway. *Crown Copyright*

Peace! What Of The Future?

LOCAL CONTROVERSY started immediately the Royal Navy took over Woodvale. In 1945 the Daily Dispatch announced that it was to close and become a civil airfield as it was of equal size to Speke and Ringway. Formby Urban District Council opposed continuing use because of the proximity of the road and railway which have, and always will be, a limiting factor. On 28 November 1945 the Air Ministry announced that Woodvale was to be kept as a Fleet Air Arm base. Southport Corporation had hopes that it would become a civil airport but at least the Admiralty had decided to hand back Ainsdale Lido (HMS Queen Charlotte) to Southport. On 1 December the Mayor of Southport, Councillor H W Barber, attacked the decision to keep the station by the FAA and demanded that it should be given to Southport. In the 1930s all local borough councils had been requested to nominate areas for possible development as civil airports and Southport nominated an area at Kew for possible development, but this was not really suitable. The chance of acquiring Woodvale would prevent any expense and put the town on the map for air travellers.

So strongly did Southport want Woodvale that they appointed a deputation to see the Air Ministry regarding their claim. Formby Council was as resolutely opposed and they published their objections on 9 January 1946 as follows:
1. Badly sited close to road and railway.
2. Not safe for civil flying in view of the fatalities already occurred.
3. Too close to Formby and too noisy.

4. Airport serving only one town is not financially viable and one serving an area would be better.

On 24 January it was announced that the Fleet Air Arm was to vacate after all but the airfield was to be handed back to the RAF and occupied by No 5 Motor Transport (MT) Company attached to the Ministry of Aircraft Production. This unit had spent the War in Sefton Park, Liverpool, and as this was now to be handed back to the City of Liverpool, Woodvale was the logical place for it. No 5 MT Company arrived on 22 February under the command of Wing Commander H C Read MBE, who also became the first post war station commander.

The MT Company had formed on 27 January 1941 for the purpose of dock clearance – transport of RAF aircraft and materials from Liverpool docks to various destinations. Other duties included transport of cased aircraft to the Aircraft Park at Southport, administered by No 47 Maintenance Unit at RAF Sealand, and from Southport to the docks. At one time cased aircraft were stored on the central reservation of the dual carriage outside Woodvale and it is assumed that these belonged to the Southport unit. The Company took over West Africa House in Water Street, Liverpool for its administrative headquarters. The original role soon expanded and it was not long until the vehicles of the unit were seen all over the country. At the time of the move work included movement of trailers to Glasgow; cased Horsa gliders from Sealand to London; Meteor aircraft in cases from Sealand to Birkenhead docks; Fifteen tonners conveying freight from the Maintenance

A group of airmen/airwomen with their Warrant Officer – all belonging to No. 5 MT Company at Woodvale.

Squadron Leader J. Wright

Unit at Heywood, Manchester to North Killingholme, Lincs and twelve cased Horsas from Sealand to Cardiff.

The unit was divided into five sections and allotted as follows:

No 1 Section	Servicing and Maintenance using 3 Hangar (Brewery Lane), the adjacent dispersal on the perimeter track and the adjacent flight offices.
No 2 Section	No 2 Hangar (Maintenance – adjacent to the main road).
No 3 Section	The two blister hangars on the railway side of the airfield together with the adjoining dispersals.
No 4 Section	Originally at Southport and reformed here on the move occupying the Technical Site including the Motor Transport bays and adjoining offices.
No 5 Section	(Workshops) No 1 Hangar (now the hardstanding), station stores, workshops, link trainer room (now West Lancs Aero Club), and other adjoining buildings.

The Commanding Officer was tasked to ensure that the signals square indicated that the airfield was closed but was to keep the runways clear of permanent obstructions so it could be used in emergency.

The unit had over five hundred vehicles and undertook 4,027 journeys in February 1946 covering 244,169 miles, the number dwindled in April to 160,377 miles and to 95,941 miles by June 1946. Four of the living sites were used by the airmen but so many lived in the Merseyside area and were allowed to live at home that one site was closed and only three stayed open. During June fifty German prisoners of war arrived to assist as many servicemen were being demobilised and a very large turnover resulted. In July Headquarters No 54 Wing notified the Company that it was to disband on 1st September and all operational commitments were to cease as from 1 August. It was intended to hand the station over to No 611 (West Lancashire) Squadron Auxiliary Air Force and priority was to be given to the formation of No 2 Motor Transport Company Detachment which was to form out of No 5 Motor Transport Company at Woodvale and continue its duties for a short period. During August three hundred and sixty four vehicles and one hundred and eighty one trailers were delivered out and the unit eventually disbanded on 15 September but there was a great amount of clearing up to be done. No 2 MT Company (Leicester East) Detachment at Woodvale, was commanded by Flight Lieutenant A Young who had arrived as detachment commander on 9 September, he was succeeded by Flying Officer H G Vallins on 28 May 1947 who was released from service on 16 December 1947. On that date the Woodvale detachment was closed, and opened up the following day at RAF Warton, located between Preston and Blackpool near Lytham St Annes, to where the main party of No 2 MT Company had proceed in the meantime.

The local councils continued their efforts to gain control. Ormskirk Council stated that as Southport was attempting to get Woodvale, it would try and get Burscough but not as an airport, but for housing. On 13 February a deputation from Southport, under Councillor Barber, met Lord Winster, the Minister of Civil Aviation. A deputation from Formby also met him to oppose the view of the Southport Councillors. The following day they were told that Woodvale was in the hands of the RAF and on 22nd it was re-occupied by No 5 MT Company.

Lancashire County Council Planning Sub-Committee agreed with the objections of the Formby Council and supported them. The Council had many airfields within its area and little effort appears to have been used in the post-war years to attempt to find a suitable alternative use for airfields. This can be seen at Burscough where it was allowed to literally fall apart until the living sites became unsafe and were demolished and the hangars slowly converted to light industrial and warehouse uses until a new industrial estate was formed out of part of the airfield. Today it remains an eyesore. In retrospect, Burtonwood would have proved to be a far better location for a North-Western regional airport than either Speke or Ringway, having a 9,000 ft long runway and acres of hardstanding and expansion areas. Instead we had a battle raging for supremacy for years, now won by Ringway.

The Air Ministry and RAF appeared to ignore the will of the local councils and with No 5 Motor Transport Squadron in occupation, announced in August that it would ultimately be the home of the newly reformed No 611 Squadron. The Air Ministry also announced that Southport should now try for Burscough as no further use was envisaged for this airfield. In September, Formby Council applied to the Air Ministry for some of the surplus accommodation for housing stating that two families of squatters were already in one hut. As some of the outlying living sites were surplus they were handed over to the Ministry of Health and administered by Formby Urban District Council as temporary accommodation until its council estates at Royal Crescent, Formby, were built.

Also in September 1946 the Air Ministry talked to Southport Corporation agreeing that some civil flying may take place if required. Two months later the Ministry of Civil Aviation also talked with Southport and put out a statement saying that Woodvale could be used as an emergency landing base when Ringway and Speke were closed due to bad weather and it was still considering the possibility of allowing charter flying.

Auxiliaries Reform – 611 Squadron

ON 10 MAY 1946 all the doubts and discussions about the future of Woodvale were dispelled as No 611 (West Lancashire) Squadron Auxiliary Air Force reformed, albeit initially at Speke and Hooton Park. The Squadron formed at RAF Hendon on 10 February 1936 as part of the pre-war expansion programme, but really began formation at Speke on 1 April 1937 when Squadron Leader G L Pilkington was commissioned as the first Commanding Officer. Auxiliary squadrons were "Part Time" being formed as a cheap extension to the regular RAF by training reserve personnel to fly "auxiliary" to the regular service. Most of the personnel were part time volunteers supported by a small full time admin and servicing staff and most flying was at weekends with annual continuation training at summer camp on regular RAF stations.

The first Squadron equipment arrived on 6 May in the form of a Hucks Starter and flying began the same month with an Avro Tutor. By the end of July Hawker Hart trainers had arrived together with the first Hawker Hart day bomber on which the Squadron was to standardise. The unit kept its Harts until April 1938 when they were replaced by Hawker Hind bombers. A fundamental change took place on New Year's Day 1939 when its role was changed to that of a fighter squadron and it was transferred to No 12 (Fighter) Group immediately receiving Spitfire I's. In August the Squadron went to Duxford, Cambs, for annual training camp and upon the outbreak of war was embodied into the full time service and soon moved to RAF Digby, Lincs, for East Coast patrols and the occasional scramble. By the end of the War it was flying Mustang IVs until disbandment on 15 August 1945 at Peterhead, Scotland.

Before disbandment the Squadron achieved considerable success destroying many enemy aircraft from its bases, which were always in the UK. Squadron pilots collected a Distinguished Service Order, fourteen Distinguished Flying Crosses, four bars to DFCs, two Distinguished Flying Medals, four bars to DFMs, and a USA Silver Star. They also had the distinction of being the first RAF aircraft to meet Russian aircraft over Berlin. Another distinction was that of the Squadron Badge which was one of the very few signed by King Edward VIII before his abdication.

With the "Cold War" continuing and the need to keep a steady reserve defence force, No 611 Squadron was reformed along with nineteen other Auxiliary squadrons. Initially it was reformed on paper at Speke, its original base, on 10 May 1946. However this was not considered to be a suitable base as it was now an expanding airport therefore it commenced to reform at Hooton Park on 26 June 1946 with the arrival of Flight Lieutenant N G Hanworth as assistant adjutant and officer in charge of training. There was, however, no intention of actually reforming at Hooton Park and Flight Lieutenant Hanworth travelled to Woodvale on 19 July to inspect the airfield and make preparations to start reforming there. Group Captain W J Leather DFC was appointed to command but lost his regular RAF rank and became a Squadron Leader Auxiliary Air Force (AuxAF). Group Captain Leather was commissioned in No 611 Squadron in 1936, and remained with it on flying duties until January 1941. In October 1940 he was awarded the DFC. For three months at the beginning of 1941 he commanded No 145 Squadron. In January 1942 he went to Air Headquarters, Far East, on Air Staff duties, and in March was posted to Air Headquarters, India, where he remained until October 1943, before going to Air Command, South East Asia, where he was at Headquarters first on Fighter Operations and later Operations.

No 5 MT Company was disbanding at Woodvale, handing over responsibility for the remaining vehicles to the Detachment of No 2 MT Company and there was much coming and going to get accommodation ready. No 611 Squadron was to take over Building No 11 on the Main Site and the Squadron officers inspected the domestic sites which were now becoming dilapidated. Squatters had moved into buildings on No 3 Site and it was decided to take over the Communal Site and the WAAF Site on North Moss Lane. To keep the squatters out the airmen were allocated two to a hut to keep them all occupied. All sites except No 1 (Communal) and the WAAF Site were de-commissioned as there were not sufficient airmen and NCOs to require them. There was to be a large contingent of regular airmen to provide maintenance and essential services for the auxiliaries who would only work weekends.

On 16 September 1946 No 611 Squadron, under the command of No 63 Group, Reserve Command at RAF Hawarden, took over control of Woodvale and provided parenting facilities for Nos 2 and 5 MT Companies. The sergeants moved into the old WAAF Mess some distance from the Officers and provided the best accommodation! However flooding on 21 September almost made them change their minds when they found themselves under six inches of water. The re-formation continued with the opening of the Town Headquarters at Everton Road, Liverpool where evening training sessions would take place, later to be shared with Liverpool University Air Squadron. On 23 October arrangements were made for the NAAFI to move to the ex-WAAF site and on 4 November 1946 the first two aircraft arrived in the form of Harvard IIB's KF223 and KF225 to form C Flight, for training.

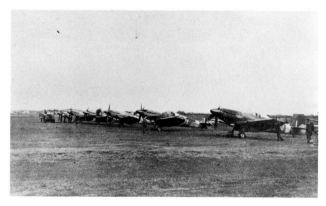

Spitfires of No. 611 Squadron lined up on the grass at Woodvale.   *Dave Vernon*

Beautifully posed view of No. 602 (City of Glasgow) Squadron AAF whilst at camp at Woodvale in July 1947. Note the buildings of the Main Site rear left.   *MoD*

Recruiting started in earnest in November with advertising on local cinema screens and in local papers and by 11 November over 100 applications had been received. By Christmas the Squadron had only two operation aircraft, two Spitfires XIV'x, and only a handful of personnel, both regular and reserve; however the traditional Christmas lunch served by the Officers to the airmen was arranged. On 1 January 1947 Squadron Leader Leather was the only auxiliary member actually assigned to the Squadron but things were looking up. Training in Harvards commenced with the third Spitfire arriving from High Ercall on 24 February and the fourth on 12 March. By March there were seven pilots, one instrument repairer, one intelligence, one equipment and one engineer auxiliaries in place and 11hrs 45 mins were flown in the Harvards. In May some noise complaints were received from residents of Formby about weekend flying, the fifth Spitfire was received and the first pilots to solo in a Spitfire Flight

Lieutenant E D H Lee DFC and Flying Officer Ormerod completed their initial conversion. On 10 June a Harvard arrived to take aerial photographs of Sir Malcolm Campbell's attempt at the World Water Speed Record on Coniston Water in the Lake District.

July 1947 was the camp period with Nos 603 (City of Edinburgh), 612 (City of Aberdeen) and 602 (City of Glasgow) Squadrons arriving for two week camps each, bringing hordes of Scotsmen to the area. This camp was marred when Flying Officer R I Reid of 602 Squadron died of injuries when he crashed into the sea off Rossall on the Flyde, apparently misjudging his height above the sea. A third Harvard arrived for No 611 Squadron, Spitfires continued to build up strength and its summer camp was held at Woodvale when at last it was able to operate as a Squadron with a rapidly growing strength. Its first activity was to fly over Wavertree Park over Liverpool Show acting as a further recruiting drive.

602 Squadron ground crew push a Spitfire 14 on the taxi way with other Spitfires and a Harvard in the background, 1947.   *MoD*

No 2611 Squadron Reforms

NO 611 SQUADRON was joined by another auxiliary unit on 1 October 1947 when No 2611 Light Anti-Aircraft Squadron Auxiliary Air Force Regiment formed under the command of Squadron Leader Black. The unit was organised on the same lines as No 611 Squadron having a few regular officers and airmen but being predominantly manned by reserve volunteers and trained by the regulars. The unit's role was to protect Woodvale against enemy air attack in the event of war. It was allotted six Bofors guns and all the ancillary back-up equipment. The Squadron met and trained at weekends and visited ranges or regular RAF stations for annual training camp but did not travel with No 611 Squadron. Squadron Leader Black was assisted by a regular adjutant, Flight Lieutenant Hardshaw and a small staff of one sergeant, two gunners, one signaller, one clerk and an armourer. The unit was housed in the Bellman hangar on the south side of the airfield by Brewery Lane, now demolished. Initially it operated from the main site on the location now used by Liverpool University Air Squadron whilst its three buildings were specially constructed adjacent to the hangar. These contained offices, stores and workshops.

A third unit moved to Woodvale in 1947 when No 186 Elementary Gliding School arrived from Hooton Park in December. The function of Elementary Gliding Schools was to train Air Training Corps cadets to fly gliders. The School had formed as No 186 (NW) Elementary Gliding School at Speke in 1944 before moving to Hooton Park and on to Woodvale. Initially flying German Grunau Baby single seater gliders under the command of Flight Lieutenant R A Tickle. These gliders were fitted with spoilers on the leading edge of the wings to prevent the wings creating lift and cadets were taught how to keep the wings straight and level on a ground slide prior to being allowed a short straight hop. This led to solo circuits but took a considerable time to teach due to the lack of two seaters. The School was manned by a staff of three or four officers in the Royal Air Force Volunteer Reserve (Training) Branch and a number of civilian instructors. Whilst at Woodvale the School totally re-equipped losing its Baby's for Cadet Mk Is and the old Mk I winches were replaced with modern self paying-on types, previously used for barrage balloons. The School operated from a (now demolished) blister hangar backing onto the Liverpool – Southport railway line and used one of the squadron offices alongside.

The single seater Mk Is were replaced by dual seater Mk IIIs but they saw little service at Woodvale except at summer camps as the school moved to Hawarden in 1951. The gliders were towed across by an Auster and whilst the school launched its gliders with winches it did utilise a Chipmunk with towing gear occasionally during Easter and Summer Camps. The arrival of the Reserve Flying School and Liverpool University Air Squadron from Hooton Park in 1951 intensified the weekend flying and made gliding unsafe and frustrating at Woodvale. It had been difficult with No 611 Squadron also operating at weekends and as No 64 Group had disbanded at Hawarden, was very quiet at weekends and the school moved there. It did, however, return to Woodvale for mid week camps during school holidays for several years as Woodvale was quieter during the week and Hawarden was used by aircraft from the factory located there. The School remained at Hawarden until its final move in 1962 to Sealand, its present home. It was renumbered and is now No 631 Volunteer Gliding School and operates virtually every weekend in the year subject to weather conditions.

King George VI gave his permission for the "Royal" prefix from 16 December 1947 and from that date the squadrons were part of the Royal Auxiliary Air Force. No 611 Squadron suffered a minor accident when Flying Officer W McCann tipped Spitfire NM794 on it's nose on landing damaging the prop and undercarriage and shock loading the engine. Fortunately there was no injury to him and the aircraft was swiftly repaired. On 8 May 1948 when the Squadron suffered its first fatality. Flying Officer Robert Griffiths and Pilot Officer Morgan took off as Red 1 and Red 2 respectively in Spitfires RN210 and RM816 to carry out practice height climbs to 25,000 feet using oxygen. Both pilots were experienced and at 21,000 feet Griffiths levelled off and advised Morgan that he was about to check his oxygen before going higher. Immediately after that his flying became irregular, yawing and steep turning eventually spinning. Morgan followed him down to 7,000 feet when he disappeared into cloud. Morgan returned to base but Griffiths crashed and burned out on marshy ground near Freckleton on the Ribble estuary. Griffiths had not attempted to bale out and was killed instantly. It was assumed that he blacked out due to oxygen failure and never recovered.

Another accident but with a happier ending occurred on

Two Grunau Babys awaiting take-off at Woodvale with No. 186 Gliding School.
B. Trunkfield

A Grunau Baby glider and Beaverette tug of No. 186 Gliding School at Woodvale. C. Coleman is driving the Beaverette with Bryan Trunkfield as crew.
B. Trunkfield

A Cadet Mk.III glider just taking off with a winch launch showing the tower and two hangars dating the photo post 1953. *APF*

3 July 1948 when Flying Officer Geldart of No 611 Squadron was on a cross country exercise to Morpeth and return. He was near Kirkby Stephen in Westmorland when he encountered sever turbulence and reduced height from 6,000 to 3,000 feet but was beginning to lose control. He knew that he was near to ground rising to 2,600 feet and decided to bale out landing safely with no more than a sprained ankle. Unfortunately the aircraft NM814 was written off in the resulting crash.

1948 continues with Squadron Leader Leather's command finishing and he handed over to Squadron Leader R P Beamont, DSO, DFC a well known war time Wing Commander who was now a test pilot with English Electric at Warton testing Vampires and the new Canberras. Camp in 1948 was held at RAF Tangmere in Sussex where the Squadron joined with regular squadrons for exercises. Now fully operational they took part in Exercise Dagger at RAF Finningley in September and acted as hosts to a Battle Of Britain open day at Woodvale on 18 September when 6,000 members of the public attended to have a look inside Woodvale – the first time it had been opened to the public. In December 1948 the Squadron flew 43 hrs 45 mins in Spitfires and 15 hrs 5 mins in Harvards and had 100 airmen.

New equipment arrived in February 1949 when thirteen Spitfire XXIIs arrived to replace the ageing XIVs. The thirteen XIVs were held for a very considerable time in storage being slowly flown out for disposal, filling Woodvale's hangars with beautiful machinery. With the new aircraft the Squadron took part in a Cheshire Air Display at Hooton Park on 10 May; four aircraft flew over Lichfield two days later when Field Marshal Lord Montgomery was reviewing the Territorial Army and six days later six aircraft carried out a mock attack as part of the Crosby Carnival celebrations. Exercise Foil at RAF Coltishall, Norfolk, in June with Fighter Command allowed the Squadron to practice interception of hostile aircraft over two weekends when it claimed two Dakotas, four Wellingtons, six B-29s, eight Mosquitoes and one Hornet. Unfortunately no camera guns were yet carried so the "kills" were difficult to

claim. Another fatal accident marred this exercise when PII R A Bailey in Spitfire PK521 returning from the exercise spun in on a glide approach and crashed into the grounds of St George's Approved School in Freshfield, Near Formby, dying instantly when he was trapped in the burning aircraft.

Grave of Flying Officer R.H.P. Griffiths at St Peter's Church, Freshfield, Formby.

Continuing Exercise

THE SQUADRON returned South for camp in 1949 travelling to RAF Thorney Island for two weeks in August but suffered engine troubles with the Spitfire XXIIs and with ten aircraft at camp they had difficulty in keeping six airworthy. Upon return in September three aircraft flew past at the Southport Battle of Britain celebrations and Woodvale again opened its gates on 17th. Over the weekend 23 and 24th they attempted to take part in Exercise Bulldog at Middle Wallop, Hants, but bad weather caused it to be cancelled. At the end of 1949 the Squadron had eleven officers (six pilots and five ground), eight airmen pilots and 127 ground crew being the largest in all the twenty one auxiliary squadrons. In November it was transferred to the direct control of Fighter Command, a step much enjoyed by Squadron members and won seventh place in the annual Auxiliary Esher Trophy.

The end of year report for 1949 shows the Squadron with thirteen Spitfire XXIIs and three Harvards. Hopes were high that Vampires may be supplied to the Squadron. There were three regular officers attached to the Squadron including Flight Lieutenant H E Walmsley DFC, as adjutant. Woodvale was commanded by Squadron Leader C G Reeves BEM acting as Camp Commandant as the task of Squadron Commander made it impossible to also command the station especially as the Squadron Commander was Auxiliary and also had a full time civilian job! The Camp Commandant/Station Commander also had two fulltime officers, an accounts officer and air traffic control officer to help him. No 2611 (Light AA) Squadron was still commanded by Squadron Leader A J Black (RAuxAF) with Flight Lieutenant Teagle acting as regular adjutant. No 2611 Squadron shared the Everton Road Town HQ. No 611 was now operationally controlled by Fighter Command through No 12 Group at RAF Newton, Notts, but domestically some aspects of administration was still under Reserve Command through No 63 Group at Hawarden in which the station remained.

1950 saw more exercises with one at Linton-on-Ouse, Yorkshire in February scrubbed due to bad weather. Not before Pilot II Raynor ran out of air pressure and landed at Burtonwood on its long runway. The record shows that his Liverpudlian accent was adulterated by Bronx from the Americans based at Burtonwood! During April the Squadron

611 Squadron Adjutant Flight Lieutenant Robin Burley watching the ground crew on a Squadron Spitfire XXII at Woodvale. *611 Squadron collection*

practised formation flying with Nos 610 and 613 Squadrons, initially at Woodvale and later at North Weald and Biggin Hill, in preparation for the Farnborough Air Show to be held in June.

Practice interceptions, Army co-operation, height climbs, formation flying, air-to-air and air-to-ground firing practice was the norm on training weekends, flying 40 hrs 10 mins in Spitfires in May. The formation practice caused a most unfortunate fatality in the Squadron on 11 June when PII Lowthian, flying from Biggin Hill, was making a formation change at about 800 feet when he collided with another aircraft flown by Flight Lieutenant Fray, the regular adjutant of No 613 Squadron, whose starboard mainplane sheared off the

Poor original showing the tented camp alongside the railway line with two blister hangars still standing and an Anson on the taxi-way. *B.H. Trunkfield*

611 Ground Crew working on a Squadron Harvard at Woodvale.
611 Squadron collection

complete tail assembly of Peter Lowthian's aircraft. He had no time to bale out and was killed instantly in the crash. He was cremated at Anfield Crematorium on 15 June.

Strong rumours were rife in June when the Squadron thought they may be called up for active duty in Korea. This was attributed to a police inspector's visit to the Squadron and saw a copy of "Mobilisation Orders for the RAuxAF" on the adjutant's desk. No call up came and the Squadron represented the RAuxAF at Farnborough in July when four aircraft from each of Nos 610, 611 and 613 Squadrons took part acting as top cover in an "Attack on Amiens Prison" set piece, this time with no accidents fortunately.

During the early 1950s Boy Entrants and Apprentices from the training schools at Halton, St Athan, Cosford and Locking spent summer camp at Woodvale. They were accommodated in a large tented camp on the railway side (west) of the airfield as the living sites were far too small for them in their current reduced state and the de-commissioned sites were falling apart and partly lived in by squatters. Each camp lasted for two weeks and three or four different groups would be accepted each year consisting of well over five hundred in each two week period. The boys arrived by special trains at Freshfield station and marched along the side of the tracks onto the airfield. The special trains were often too long for the platform and the level crossing was closed for half an hour as the train was emptied or filled. Fortunately at that time there were not too many houses on the seaward side of the crossing. Whilst at Woodvale, they flew in Chipmunks, Tiger Moths, Ansons and Oxfords, shot on the Altcar Rifle Ranges and carried out leadership exercises on the Altcar Army ranges. Woodvale was the only station to receive these large numbers for many years, probably due to the fact that it was well placed for Altcar, was now comparatively quiet having little week-day activity and it's capacity for providing an assortment of activities. The tented camp was vast and was also utilised by Air Training Corps cadets and University Air Squadrons, both of which also visited Woodvale in the summer, with Leeds UAS being in residence in July 1950. The first of 421 Apprentices arrived on 10 June 1953 for example.

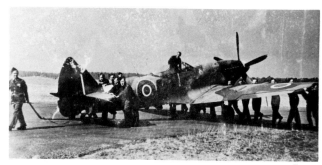

611 Squadron Spitfire at Woodvale circa 1950 *611 Squadron collection*

Spitfires Mk XVI (nearest) and FXXII both of 611 Squadron at Woodvale. *Dave Vernon*

611 Pilots examine a target drogue after air to air firing at summer camp at RAF Thorney Island 1949. *611 Squadron collection*

611 Squadron ground crew at camp at RAF Tangmere 1948. Warrant Officer Lawrence standing centre. *611 Squadron collection*

611 and 613 (City of Manchester) Spitfires being refuelled at Summer Camp.

611 Squadron collection

Whilst Woodvale was full of visitors No 611 Squadron took off for camp at Sylt which was the Armament Practice Camp for the British Army on the Rhine (BAOR). Eight Spitfires and two Harvards made the trip, and after several malfunctions then aircraft arrived with the ground crew being ferried by two Hastings and a York from Woodvale. This camp had no regular RAF crews to assist maintenance and the Squadron stood totally on its own feet for the first time doing all servicing unaided and gaining valuable experience. All pilots fired air-to-ground and air-to-air using up 16,322 rounds. Upon return further exercises took up weekends and the 1950 open day at Woodvale saw 4,000 people attend on a wet day but the flying continued with No 611 Squadron carrying out a practice shoot up of Hooton Park whilst No 610 Squadron

from Hooton Park did the same to the crowds at Woodvale. Total profit for the RAF Benevolent Fund for the day was £57.00.

Later in 1950 exercises were held at Aldergrove in Northern Ireland, Woodvale and Linton-on-Ouse, the Fighter Command station to which the Squadron was affiliated. At Aldergrove the Squadron undertook many scrambles and claimed four "enemy" aircraft destroyed on 14 October and eight the following day. At Woodvale, Exercise Emperor brought the station up to an operational level and 611 Squadron was joined by No 502 Squadron in defensive air patrols. Due to pressure at work Squadron Leader Beamont relinquished control of the Squadron and handed over to Squadron Leader H R P Pertwee DFC in November.

Jets Arrive

1950 AND 1951 saw a large building programme get underway with the extension of the main runway (04/22) in a northerly direction to give 600 feet of extra length, the construction of a fourth hangar next to the main hangar on the Main Site, installation of new fuel storage tanks for Avtur, jet fuel. Members of No 611 Squadron were now expectant that jets were on their way and the first Meteor T7's arrived on 4 April when two brand new Meteors were flown in from the Gloster factory airfield at Moreton Valence (Gloucs). Prior to that the Squadron was flying more air firing exercises with towed sea targets off Anglesey and with regular squadrons at Horsham St Faith and also interception training with the Auxiliary radar station unit at Hack Green, Cheshire. Squadron flying continued with the twelve Spitfires and three Harvards whilst conversion training started in earnest on the Meteors. The CO, Squadron Leader Pertwee, was the first to solo in a Meteor T7 on 13 April and a third T7 arrived from Leeming, to accelerate conversion, later in the month. However as the runway was still being lengthened this process was made very difficult with only 1,600 yards being available.

May 1951 was an intense month for the Squadron. Talks commenced regarding moving the Squadron to Hooton Park to join up with No 610 Squadron already in residence there even though new hangar accommodation had just been provided together with the longer main runway. The first two Meteor F4's arrived on 17 May with three more by the end of the month and all the Spitfires had been put up for disposal as No

611 Squadron Pilots lined up before Coronation fly past 1953 at Hooton Park. Centre: Wing Commander Westlake, CO of RAF Hooton Park.

611 Squadron collection

611 Squadron and Woodvale joined the jet age. Teething troubles with a much more sophisticated aircraft were inevitable and Flight Lieutenant Parker and Sergeant Griffiths landed short of the runway in a T7 on 2 June damaging the port nacelle and wing and Flight Lieutenant Parker landed wheels up eight days later in a F4. Although nothing to do

Meteor T7 WF770 'W' of 611 Squadron at Woodvale circa 1953.

611 Squadron collection

Oxford NJ305 of Western Sector maintained by 611 Squadron before the unit moved to Woodvale.   *P.H.Butler*

with his flying Flight Lieutenant Parker was posted to RAF Chivenor and replaced by Flight Lieutenant J H Pearce as adjutant on 20 June. At the end of the month Fighter Command decided to move No 611 Squadron to Hooton Park and join No 610 (City of Chester) Squadron already there and forming part of the Wing.

Flying was reduced to a minimum as preparations were made for the move and on 8 July the HQ function at Woodvale ceased as the Squadron transferred to Hooton Park. The Squadron was taking over accommodation being vacated by No 19 Reserve Flying School which was swopping places and moving to Woodvale but was not so advanced with its preparations and hindered the move. However by mid July the transfer was complete and No 611 called all its members up for three months continuous training on the new jet aircraft. At the time of the move the Squadron was commanded by Squadron Leader H R P Pertwee, DFC who was a regular with three other regular and eight auxiliary officers, seven sergeant pilots, 68 regular airmen and NCOs and 73 auxiliary airmen with 10 NCOs. The Squadron had six Meteor F4's, three T7, three Spitfire XXIIs and three Harvards. The Squadron also maintained an Oxford for Western Sector based at Squires Gate. The Squadron did not like their F4's as they

were old and unreliable and not much faster than their Spitfires with an inferior duration. However after the concentrated three month work up they were very much more professional and operationally capable and started to replace their ageing F4's with F8's in March 1952.

Woodvale had fleetingly come into the jet age but lost its jets almost as soon as they arrived although its facilities had been updated but this allowed three resident units from Hooton Park to move across the Mersey to Woodvale. These units were University of Liverpool Air Squadron, No 19 Reserve Flying School and the THUM Flight. No 663 Army Co-Operation Squadron was also due to move across from Hooton Park and a canvas bessoneau hangar was erected especially for it in November 1951 but the Squadron stayed at Hooton Park. It was ultimately removed by a party from No 3 MU Milton in February 1954. A new D4 Link Trainer was fitted in the Link Trainer building, (now occupied by West Lancs Aero Club), and seven day a week flying was introduced which stretched the RAF controllers beyond their capacity and civilian controllers had to be brought in for the first time. In July 1951 No 3611 Sqn RAUXAF, a mobile Ground Control Interception Unit was based on the airfield. The annual Battle of Britain At Home this year saw 6,009 people attending.

Liverpool University Air Squadron

UNIVERSITY OF Liverpool Air Squadron had re-formed in December 1950 under Squadron Leader J H (Paddy) Gaston who had formed part of the first course of RAF pilots to train in the USA after America joined World War Two. Initially the Squadron had no aircraft and was housed in a town headquarters at 19 Bedford Street, Liverpool before moving to the Everton Road HQ also used by 611, 2611 and 3611 Squadrons on different evenings. The Squadron held its first annual camp at RAF Fazakerley, Liverpool a Balloon station with no airfield, and utilised the Harvards of Nos 610 and 611 Squadrons at Hooton Park whilst waiting for its own aircraft. Before receiving aircraft at Hooton Park it moved to Woodvale on 14 July 1951 where it received its first Chipmunk T10's.

The first notable incident was an accident on 14 December 1951 when Chipmunk WB552 crash landed in the forced landing practice area when it's engine failed to pick up during a practice forced landing. The aircraft suffered considerable damage but the instructor and student escaped without injury. Easter Camp in 1952 was held at Woodvale using a Harvard borrowed from No 611 Squadron. Liverpool University Air Squadron is the longest serving unit at Woodvale having remained there forty years – still being there as this is written. The Squadron flies throughout the university term on a student opportunity basis with the maximum attendance at weekends. Originally the students flew one hundred and twenty hours averaging forty per annum. Night flying for the senior students took place on one night per week during the winter term but this was discontinued as an economy measure and now only instructors fly occasionally at night for continuity training. Ground training evenings are held at Town Headquarters every Thursday evening, originally at Everton Road but now from a purpose built building in the University campus area. During the Christmas and Easter vacations two camps were held, each lasting a week and held at Woodvale. In the summer the Squadron goes to an active RAF station for a two week camp for consolidation and extra experience, the first being held at RAF Upwood, Cambs, in 1952.

One of the highlights of the year is the annual competition between this and other University Air Squadrons for various efficiency trophies. These competitions have been modified and changed in recent years but for many years the squadrons of Manchester, Birmingham and Queen's (Belfast) and the University of Wales competed, with Liverpool, for the de Havilland Trophy. This was a regional competition with the winner going to the Central Flying School. then at RAF Little Rissington, to compete in the Hack Trophy against the winners of the other regional heats. The de Havilland Trophy has spent much of its time at Woodvale, University of Liverpool Air Squadron holding it during the first year it was presented in 1953 and again in 1955, 1959, 1961, 1962 and 1963. The Trophy now contested is the Reid Trophy which has been won by the Squadron in 1972, 1975, 1978, 1980, 1981, 1986 and 1990.

One of the main aims of the University Air Squadrons is to recruit graduates into the RAF and members gain their preliminary flying badge reducing the number of hours required when training for their wings in the RAF. It also provides a unit for undergraduates who have won RAF cadetships where their take an acting RAF officer rank whilst at University and are paid and have their tuition fees paid by the RAF, joining the RAF upon graduation. The three basic

Air Commodore W.S. Hebdon, AOC No. 63 Group, presents the new LUAS badge to the Commanding Officer Squadron Leader P.N. Farlow at the Everton Road HQ on 13 November 1954.

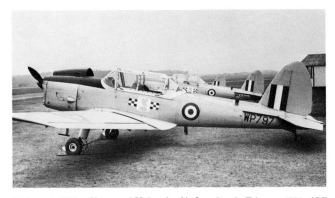

Chipmunk T10's of Liverpool University Air Squadron in February 1971. *APF*

aims of the University Air Squadrons remain to this day and are:

> To boost interest in the RAF among University Students.

> To give selected training to undergraduates and a taste of service life − particularly flying.

> To give pre-entry training to RAF sponsored undergraduates who have opted for an RAF career.

The first student to solo was Officer Cadet E G Derbyshire. Squadron Leader Gaston was posted out on 10 April 1952, Flight Lieutenant W G Bennett taking temporary command until 14 July when Squadron Leader P N Farlow assumed command. One of the Squadron's aircraft took part in the Coronation Review of the RAF at Odiham in May 1953.

The Squadron was controlled by Headquarters No 63 Group, Home Command based at Hawarden, and its AOC Air Commodore W S Hebden, presented the unit badge to Squadron Leader Farlow on 12 November 1954. the badge comprises a Cormorant holding in its beak a branch of seaweed (as in the arms of Liverpool) and standing on a book to suggest learning. The motto under reads "Studiis divisi - volando sociati" − "In Studies they are divided − by flying they are united". The Badge was approved and signed by Her Majesty Queen Elizabeth II. The Squadron operated from its buildings in front of the pair of hangars on the Main Site until 1990 when it moved to new premises on the site of the Manchester University Air Squadron building, where a new purpose built HQ has been constructed. Normally four or five Chipmunk T10 aircraft were operated from Wednesday to Sunday with a stand down on Monday and Tuesday. From 1954 two Harvards were attached to the Squadron and they took them to camp at

Squadron Leader L.J. Cook photographed with staff and students before his tragic death in April 1956. Photograph April 1955. *Liverpool Daily Post and Echo*

RAF Booker, near Marlow, Bucks, in 1954 where they had access to eleven Chipmunks as Booker was an Elementary Flying Training School with Chipmunks. The Harvards stayed on strength going to camp at RAF Upwood in 1955 and RAF Booker again in 1956, losing them when they were withdrawn in March 1957.

Tragedy struck LUAS on 15 April 1956 when Squadron Leader L J Cook, Officer Commanding, died in a crash when Chipmunk WD351 crashed near Lydiate, a few miles to the East of Woodvale. His passenger Flying Officer John A Pinnell escaped with minor injuries. Squadron Leader Cook, only thirty one years old, was cremated at Anfield Crematorium on 18 April. His command taken over by Flight Lieutenant A J McCracken pending the posting in of Squadron Leader D H Simmons.

Squadron Leader Norman Jones receiving the de Havilland Trophy from the Lord Mayor of Liverpool outside the Squadron HQ at Woodvale on 20 April 1960.

19 Reserve Flying School

The second unit to arrive in 1951 was No 19 Reserve Flying School. This was a civilian manned unit responsible for keeping trained a nucleus of pilots, navigators and observers in case of war or emergency. The School had approximately five Tiger Moths, ten Chipmunk T10s, two Oxfords and sixteen Ansons at the date of the move from Hooton Park and was commanded by Squadron Leader C G Reeves MBE who was also acting as Station Commander. Squadron Leader F Chapman was Chief Instructor and Flight Lieutenant B Twitchett Chief Flying Instructor. J W Jefferson was Chief Ground Instructor and Tony Neil was link trainer instructor. The School was manned by civilian pilots and instructors from Short Bros and Harland under contract to the Air Ministry. The School occupied the old Armoury (now site of 10 AEF), canteen, civilian contractors office (now site of MASUAS) and the offices on the site of the current LUAS building.

The first concept of the Reserve Flying School in the immediate post war period was that the RAF would establish Reserve Centres near major centres of population. These centres were initially responsible for the ground training and administration of the RAFVR aircrews, with flying training taking place at civil operated airfields. The division of responsibility was not particularly successful so the aircrew attended the Reserve Flying School for ground and flying training. Thus the ground training was carried out by the operating company running the Reserve Flying School. Ground and air training could be co-ordinated, however the

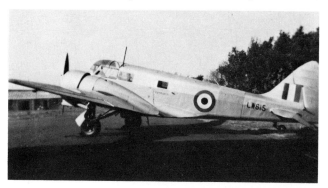

Oxford T2 LW815 operated with both 19RFS and CFCCU in the early 1950's.

Chipmunk T10 WP972 operated with 19RFS. Seen here adjacent to the new 'Meteor' hangar with LUAS's HQ behind.

A Tiger Moth of Leeds UAS landing on the grass. The UAS was on summer camp at Woodvale and three more Tigers can be seen parked on the grass with a Chipmunk in front of the maintenance hangar. At this date July 1950, the workshops had not been built alongside the maintenance hangar.   *P.A. Cross*

Reserve Centres were still responsible for the administration appertaining to the personnel of the RAFVR. When No 19 RFS was formed at Hooton Park it catered for the flying training of the Liverpool area (RAF Fazakerley Reserve centre) for pilots, navigators and signallers and also for the flying training of navigators and signallers of the Manchester area (RAF Bowlee Reserve Centre). The ground training was then carried out by the Reserve centres whilst the pilots attended Barton airfield for their flying training.

When No 19 Reserve Flying School moved to Woodvale, the ground training was transferred from the Reserve centres to the reserve Flying School and, due to a re-organisation of contracts, the pilots of RAF Bowlee also attended the Reserve Flying School. The individual aircrews were required to attend fifteen days annual continuous training and a requisite number of non-continuous training during the year. They were required to obtain forty hours flying per year which was ideally completed as twenty hours during continuous training and twenty hours during non-continuous training. The School was open seven days a week and night flying was carried out on one night per week during the winter months. The type of training was both a revision of previous RAF training and also included new concepts and operational requirements. As training progressed the type of flight became more interesting with cross country flights to Jersey and Guernsey, to selected airfields in Germany and exercises in co-operation with merchant shipping. The Anson T21s were well equipped having Gee, Air Position Indicators, Air Direction Finding Equipment, Drift meters, Distant Reading Compasses and full dinghy equipment. Some of the RAFVR members were called up to regular service and saw action in Korea.

In the heyday of the RAFVR the Reserve Flying Schools were further enlarged with courses of instruction in the following:

1 Pilots instructors course (to obtain RAF Instructor's category).

2 Ab-initio training to interim wings standard

3 Ab-initio training for Air Traffic Control Officers. (These officers attended lectures at night and weekends and obtained their practical experience under the guidance of the ATC officers employed by the RFS)

Anson of 19RFS prepares to leave on a training flight, left to right: Russ Jones, Ted Perrins, ? , Dennis Crossley, ? .

G.A. Peakman

Instructors included John Formby, Gordon Hargreaves, Ginger Irving, Messrs Sharp, Briggs, Chapman and Wheeler, all employed by Short Bros and Harland and also flying with other units simultaneously located at Woodvale.

No 19 Reserve Flying School had a very good safety record considering the large number of flying hours, especially as most were for training. Unfortunately this record was blemished when Flying Officer "Red" Limpett-Lowe crashed in a Chipmunk on 20 December 1952 south of Formby. The reason for the accident was given to carburettor icing, causing a forced landing. Fortunately this was not fatal and although the aircraft was written off, the pilot was OK.

With increased defence cuts it was deemed that Reserve Flying Schools were too expensive to run and not required as a part of our reserve forces. Accordingly all Reserve Flying Schools were disbanded on 20 June 1954 and the aircraft withdrawn.

19RFS Ansons lined up at Woodvale in 1953. Codes appear to be '36', '34', '40', '38' and '37'.

P.H. Butler

Thum Flight Arrives

The third unit to move across from Hooton Park to Woodvale in July 1951 was the THUM Flight. The initials stood for "T" temperature and "HUM" humidity as it was a meteorological flight. The Air Ministry contract for the operation of the THUM Flight was placed with Short Bros and Harland Ltd, Flying Schools Division in early 1951. The task had hitherto been carried out by the RAF using Mosquito aircraft.

THUM Flight, in its new civilian operated role, was formed at Hooton Park in April 1951 alongside No 19 Reserve Flying School, and other Air Ministry commitments already the responsibility of Shorts. It was decided that Mosquito aircraft would not continue in service, and the Flight was originally equipped with three Griffon 66 powered Spitfire PRXIX aircraft, PM549, PM577 and PM652.

The task was to gather information on conditions existing in the upper atmosphere, for onward transmission to the Central Forecasting Office, then at Dunstable. The data to be collected during the climb to 300 millibars (approximately 30,000 ft) over a point three miles north of Worcester. Top of the climb to be reached by 0900 hours GMT daily.
The pilot was to be responsible for reporting wet and dry bulb temperatures at 540, 1040 and 1540 feet above mean sea level, and then at 900 millibars and every 50 millibars up to 300 millibars, aircraft to be levelled at each height. Additionally, reports to be made on inversions, isothermals, haze, visibility, cloud types and amount, ice formation, contrails, turbulence, and present weather − not exactly a joy ride!

The met instruments fitted were a Balanced Bridge Psychrometer and Aneroid Barometer, the only air to navigation being an eight channel VHF radio.

The first THUM Flight commander was Mr T D Carter (Ex Flight Lieutenant, RAFRO) who carried out the first practice flight in PM549 on 17 April. There followed a few days of intensive preparation, flying practice and Meteorological study. The first operational met sortie was made by Mr Carter in PM549 on 28 April 1951. It was soon found that the task, to be carried out under all weather conditions in an aircraft not originally envisaged for high intensity instrument flying, called for the utmost skill and determination.

On 29 April 1951, Mr T V Heyes DFC (Flight Lieutenant RAFVR) was seconded from No 19 Reserve Flying School to assist with the THUM Flight, carrying out his first flight on 6 May. At the end of May, Mr Carter left the Flight to take over No 5 CAACU (shortly to be seen at Woodvale), a new Shorts contract at RAF Llanbedr, Merioneth, North Wales. His place was taken until the end of July by Mr Ackers, who then took up a test pilot's post at Sir W G Armstrong Whitworth Aircraft Ltd.

During July it was decided that the aircraft establishment should be increased to four Spitfires to allow a margin of safety in serviceability due to the gradual reduction of spares for this type of aircraft. PM631 was flown in to make the quartet. During this month came the upheaval when No 19 RFS, Liverpool University Air Squadron and the THUM Fight moved across to Woodvale, swopping places with No 611 Squadron. It was a credit to the Flight that no climbs were lost due to the move, involving as it did changes of staff and homes, and engagement of almost a complete new ground staff. The authorization book shows that on 13 July, Mr Akers, in PM652, took off from Hooton Park and landed after the climb at Woodvale.

Tommy Heyes reunited with his dog after returning from a Thum Flight climb in 1953.
F Chapman

Mrs Jackson and Mrs Lewis packing parachutes at Woodvale in 1956.
F Chapman

Tommy Heyes after taking over the Thum Flight photographed shortly before his death, at Church Pulverbach in Spitfire PR XIX PM628. *F Chapman*

Mr Gordon Hargreaves (Flying Officer RAFVR) took over from Mr Akers at the time of the move to Woodvale and continued as Flight Commander, Tommy Hayes continuing in the role of THUM pilot and RFS instructor.

In late 1951, a case was put by the Company for an additional radio which could be used in case of failure of the installed FR 1430 or its associated generators, power pack etc. Eventually in 1952 the aircraft were modified to take an Ecko CE 1140 with its own 12 volt accumulator for use purely as an emergency standby. It was whilst PM652 was being flown into St Athan for this modification by a pilot newly attached to the Flight, that the undercarriage collapsed presumably due to a heavy landing. this aircraft was replaced by PS853 in April 1952.

On 4 May 1952 tragedy first struck the Unit. Gordon Hargreaves took off for the routine ascent in PM549 in bad weather conditions, but returned to base with radio trouble. He rejoined the circuit but was killed when the aircraft stalled and spun in whilst turning onto the final approach.

It then fell to Tommy Heyes to take over command of the Flight and carry on unaided for a period of over five weeks. He was relieved for a few days by another company pilot, Mr Allum and Mr G Irving was trained to take on THUM Flight duties, making his first operational climb on 23 June 1952. In July PM628 was flown in to replace the crashed PM549. Soon after this, it was decided that the pilots should work as an integral part of No 19 RFS staff to spread the load and make better allowance for sickness etc. Accordingly Mr Heyes and Mr Irving were joined by John Formby (Flight Lieutenant RAFRO) who carried out his first Spitfire practice flight on Battle Of Britain Day, 20 September 1952 when 7076 people attended. These three pilots carried on through 1953 with an almost 100% record of climbs, and on to March 1954 with precise regularity. It was possible to set your watch in Freshfield at 08.00 when the Spitfire could be heard to take off.

On 4 March 1954 came the second tragedy, when Tommy Heyes was killed whilst returning from a climb in PM628. He was a brilliant pilot and had carried out 426 met climbs, and had twice been put forward as a candidate for an award for his THUM Flight work. The accident occurred whilst near Church Pulverbach, to the South of Shrewsbury in the first visual flight conditions encountered for days, and after the pilot had radioed that he was abandoning the aircraft due to a rough running engine. It appears however, from contemporary newspaper reports that he realised that he was near the village and a school so stayed with the aircraft to steer it away from the houses and died in the crash. There is a plaque in the church at Church Pulverbach erected by Tommy's wife, Iris, and friends.

The commemorative plaque inside the church at Church Pulverbach, Shropshire. *APF*

End of Reserve Flying School

No 19 Reserve Flying School closed in July and before that Mr Irving left Shorts. John Formby took over command of the Flight and carried on unaided from 23 March 1954 to 3 July 1954 except for a period of five days. PM651 was delivered towards the end of March 1954 as a replacement for PM628. PM651's career was short lived, for on 14 April whilst being flown to the ascent point by Mr Formby, overspeeding and low oil pressure were experienced at a height of less than 1000 feet. These symptoms increased, and a successful forced landing was made at Halfpenny Green near Wolverhampton. On investigation it was found that a grain of sand had caused the oil dilution button to be jammed in, thus causing petrol to be pumped into the oil supply. This aircraft was not re-issued for flying duties and went to grace the entrance to RAF Hucknall, Notts. Its place in the Flight was taken, in June 1954, by PS915.

Mr John C M Wood (Flying Officer RAFRO) joined the Flight in June 1954 and flew his first met operational sortie on 4 July 1954. The comparative lack of engine troubles in previous years did not hold good through 1954. Another forced landing was made on 22 July, this time by Mr Wood in PS853 on the disused airfield at Calveley, Cheshire. It was found that the carburettor of this aircraft had failed, after replacement the aircraft was flown back to Woodvale.

On 17 November 1954, John Formby in PM577 landed at RAF Valley following the climb, a normal diversion caused by bad weather at base. As usual the aircraft was soon surrounded by enthusiastic young airmen, brought up entirely in the "Jet Age", to gaze at this piston engined steed of the past generation. Unfortunately they then proceeded to refuel with the jet engine fuel AVTUR, at which the engine luckily jibbed just prior to take off.

Christmas Eve 1954 was not the start of a particularly happy Christmas for John Formby. When nearing the top of the climb at 30,000 feet, the canopy of PS915 disintegrated, then pilot was momentarily knocked unconscious, by the resultant explosive decompression. However, control was regained, and some twenty minutes later a very cold and chattering pilot stepped from the aircraft at Woodvale, to find that the electric tea urn had broken! The temperature at 30,000 feet on that day was 110 degrees F below freezing.

It was decided that PM652, the last remaining Spitfire

John Formby taking Met readings in an 'arranged' photograph in front of Spitfire PRXIX PM577 in 1957. *John Formby*

PRXIX available, should be moved to Woodvale. On 11 January 1955 it was collected by Mr Formby from RAF Colerne, but over the Wrekin at 6,500 feet, PM652 decided to throw a con-rod through a cylinder side. A forced landing was made at RAF High Ercall albeit this time with the undercarriage retracted. A close thing, successfully accomplished through the aid of intimate knowledge of the area gained during numerous flights on this route. A moment of light relief came when a complaint was made about damage to the airfield grass, and attempts by the pilot to remove the hood from the aircraft were resisted. This was badly needed back at base, and Mr Formby was quite prepared to take it back with him by train, explanations that the nearest known serviceable hood was at Kuala Lumpur, were of no avail and it had to be left to come through normal channels.

Frustrations continued into 1955 when the aircraft were all grounded on 8 May whilst investigations were made into a batch of carburettors which were thought to be malfunctioning due to long and incorrect storage. These were the first flights actually lost through unserviceability in the four years which the unit had been operating.

In May 1955 Mr Wood left to take up helicopter flying abroad and his place was taken by Mr P Brooke (Master Pilot RAFVR). In August came the good news that John Formby had been awarded the L G Groves Memorial Award for Air.

Spitfire PRXIX being marshalled in 1955. *F Chapman*

Spitfire PRXIX in a dismantled state at RAF Cosford after its forced landing at High Ercall, Shropshire in January 1955.

Meteorological Observers for the year ended 31 July 1955, having completed 462 sorties at that time. Mr Brooke left in December 1955 leaving John Formby alone again until he was joined by Eric A Richards (Flight Sergeant RAFVR) on 29 February 1956.

In early 1956 it was decided that as the spares backing for Spitfire PRXIX's was getting critical, they should be replaced by other aircraft. Accordingly in January 1956 a Spitfire F24 (VN315) was sent in for flight trials, but was found to be unsuitable for the task. In April 1956 a master stroke of planing was devised in the chain of command to ease the spares position. The idea was to withdraw one of the four established aircraft to hold as spare "Fit to Fly" backing in storage. Accordingly PM577 was flown to RAF High Ercall on 15 May. At a later date, when this aircraft was urgently required it was found that it had been broken up. An interesting side light is that an enthusiastic aircraft spotter had seen the remains of this aircraft on a Queen Mary on a quiet Midlands road, traced it back, and reported it to the THUM Flight.

A Mosquito TT 35 was sent in for flight trials in July 1956. the trials proved satisfactory, the Air Ministry decided that they would replace the Spitfires probably in April 1957.

Earlier in the 1950s the USAF had requested permission to use Woodvale in co-operation with the TA for parachute dropping exercises. Over the weekend 28 and 29 June 1952 Fairchild C-82 Packet aircraft arrived for exercises with 46th Parachute Brigade TA. A week later seven C-82s arrived and the station provided accommodation for 300 parachutists in the annual tented camp by the railway. Exercise "Short Drop" involved the aircraft and men being taken and dropped over the airfield at Burtonwood. In September twelve C-82s arrived from Germany, collected 308 troops and took them to

Germany to partake in Exercise "Holdfast". More US aircraft, this time in the shape of the later version known as the C-119, were seen parked on the perimeter track by the railway in June 1953 again operating with 46th Para Brigade in Exercise "Bung Ho" in Germany. Again the troops and aircrew were accommodated at Woodvale prior to the arrival of the Apprentice and Boy Entrant Camps.

A rehabilitation programme was commenced on the remaining buildings throughout 1952. The buildings had been designed and constructed to last through the war only and were now ten years old and suffering signs of age and neglect. The only sites still in use off the airfield were the Communal and ex-WAAF Sites and all were reroofed and decorated with improvements in toilets and electricity supply. By the end of 1953 the station had a strength of two Officers, three Warrant Officers, six Senior NCOs and 91 corporals and below. These personnel were running the station and ancillary units whilst the individual units, 2611 Squadron, University of Liverpool Air Squadron, 19 Reserve Flying School, THUM Flight and Manchester University Air Squadron all had their own officers whilst servicing was undertaken by the permanent RAF members. Aircrew and instructors for 19 RFS and aircrew for the THUM Flight being civilian provided under contract by Short Bros and Harland.

1954 saw the usual round of camps starting with the first party of 638 in the middle of June. No 19 RFS disbanded but in May there was another USAF exercise with members of 16th Airborne Division and 13th Para Battalion operating from Woodvale again. With the RFS Ansons gone three extra Ansons were flown in to give Boy Entrants air experience flying, followed by the ATC camps in August, which in turn, were followed by Apprentices from RAF Halton at the end of

Spitfire PRXIX PM631 with two Ansons parked beyond, Woodvale 1956.
John Formby

PS853 taking off in mid summer with the tented camp clearly in the background.
Flight International

PM631 outside the hangar at Woodvale in 1956.
John Formby

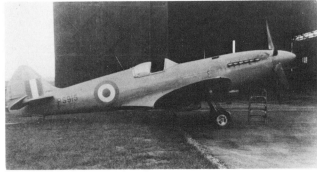

Spitfire PRXIX PS915 at rest at Woodvale circa 1956.
John Formby

Spitfire PRXIX PS853 taking off with the Old Golf Club House in the background. Once used as the Officers' Mess it was now derelict and soon to be demolished. Photo 1957. *Southport Visitor*

Woodvale's own station flight Anson seen here in 1957 by the hangar adjacent to Brewery Lane (now demolished). After vacation by No. 2611 Squadron the hangar was used for spraying aircraft and storage.

H.M. The Queen Mother alighting from a Queens Flight BAe146 at Woodvale on 12 April 1991 en route to Aintree Race Course.

John C. Daly, Visitor Series of Newspapers

the month. Intensive preparations were made in July for a visit by HRH The Queen Mother who was due on 23rd of the month to present the Colours to the Manchester Regiment at Harrington Barracks, Formby. Unfortunately her itinerary took her by road instead of flying and she missed Woodvale.

Several RAF Regiment Auxiliary squadrons came for summer camp in 1955 when nine Squadrons arrived each for a weeks camp. The Squadrons spent one week at Woodvale and then moved to an Army range for live firing during the second week. This year a royal visit did occur when HRH The Princess Margaret arrived by air for a visit to the St John's Ambulance Brigade in Southport. Another Royal visitor was HRH The Duke of Edinburgh when he flew in en route to Martin Mere Wild Life reserve, near Southport, in April 1979 in a Queen's Flight Andover. The flight from Woodvale was filmed by a crew for the television programme "Magpie" featuring an article on the Queen's Flight. 1991 has seen probably more Royal visitors than ever before with HRH The Queen Mother flying in on 12 April to open a new stand at Aintree Race Course, followed on 8 May by HRH The Princess Margaret for a tour of South Sefton; both flying in BAe 146 aircraft of the Queen's Flight. HRH The Duke of York visited in June and the Royal family and other VIP's are using Woodvale more regularly rather than causing security problems at Liverpool (Speke) Airport.

Manchester University Air Squadron

Manchester University Air Squadron arrived at Woodvale from Barton, Manchester on 14 March 1953. As with the move of No 611 Squadron to Hooton Park to join No 610 Squadron, it was deemed sensible to have two close University Air Squadrons to operate from a common base. The Squadron had reformed post war at Barton during early 1946 flying Tiger Moths. The Tiger Moths were replaced by Chipmunks before the move and they brought five Chipmunks to Woodvale taking over the accommodation previously used by No 2611 Squadron on the Main Site, with No 2611 moving across the airfield to new accommodation close to the hangar backing onto Brewery Lane. These building being specially built for

One of Manchester University Air Squadrons' early Chipmunks WD322/K seen at Woodvale in 1954.

2611 Squadron. Only three months after moving to Woodvale, a Chipmunk (WD326) was lost on Waltham Moor on the Pennines killing Flying Officer K B Wallace and Pilot Officer F Reddish.

The Squadron had the same task as that of Liverpool University Air Squadron and have won the de Havilland Trophy in 1956, 1957, 1958, 1960, 1962 and 1966, winning the Hack trophy in 1960, 1982, 1985, 1987, and 1989 and the Reid trophy in 1971, 1973, 1977, 1982, 1984, 1985, 1987, 1989 and 1991.

Woodvale had now a settled series of Commanding Officers; on 4 February 1954 Squadron Leader E D Griffiths took over from Squadron Leader D W Baldwin who had commanded since September 1951. No 19 RFS closed in June 1954 but weekend flying was still very busy to the extent that No 186 Gliding School moved to Hawarden in December 1952. Another unit to operate from Woodvale arrived in 1952 known as the Civilian Fighter Control Co-operation Unit (CFCCU). It had been based at RAF Fazakerley, Liverpool but used Oxfords and Ansons from 19 RFS and the Woodvale Station Flight as targets for its controllers. It is uncertain whether this unit had any aircraft of its own and is more likely to have used Woodvale based aircraft as its targets. This unit disbanded in 1957 with all the Royal Auxiliary Air Force.

Western Sector Flight moved from Squires Gate to Woodvale during 1956. It was set up for as two fold duty; one was to give flying experience to pilots serving ground tours in the North West but, secondly, to liaise with and provide

Grounded by mist, four of MUAS's Chipmunks waiting for the weather to clear − October 1968. Note the early Squadron markings.

APF

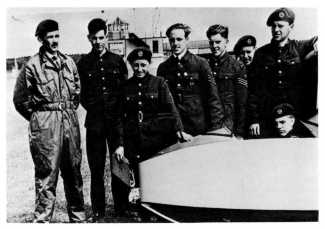

Taken around the time of the move to Hawarden members of 186 Gliding School stand by a Cadet MkIII glider with Bryan Trunkfield on far left.

Recieving the title deed of the Freedom of Entry to Southport in a silver holder from the Mayor (Councillor F.E. Thornley). Centre: AVM BC Yarde CVO, CBE, Commandant in General of the RAF Regiment and Inspector of Ground Combat Training. Right: Squadron Leader A.R. Poole DSO, DFC, CO of 2611 Squadron. *Southport Visitor via K. McCabe*

transport to HQ Western Sector located at Squires Gate, across the Ribble Estuary. Western Sector appears to have been a reserve unit acting under control of No 64 Group at Hawarden and the Flight had Oxfords, Ansons and Meteors. It formed originally as a civilian unit at Squires Gate operated by the lancashire Aircraft Corporation Limited with Shorts Bros taking over the job at Woodvale in 1956. Like the CFCCU this unit probably borrowed most of its aircraft from other Woodvale based aircraft. This unit only survived a few years

On a wet day in June 1956 No. 2611 Squadron received the Freedom to Entry to Southport. The ceremony took place on Southport Promenade outside the end of the pier and the march past was down Lord Street.
Southport Visitor via K. McCabe

and was caught in the infamous and savage defence cuts in 1957 disbanding on 25 October 1957.

No 982 Signals Unit arrived in May 1955 operating until disbandment on 1 March 1957 as another victim of the review. No doubt this unit operated in conjunction with both Western Sector Flight and the CFCCU.

The first phase of the 1956 Halton apprentice camp arrived in May followed in June by the first auxiliary camp staying for one week before moving to the range at Trawsfynydd. They were followed by nine further squadrons undertaking the first phase of annual training. July saw the first of two hundred and sixty eight ATC cadets arrive for their camp under canvas, all visitors not finally leaving until September. A great honour was conferred to No 2611 Squadron on 16 July when it received the Freedom of Entry into Southport. Undeterred by the continual rain, the parade formed up opposite the pier entrance on the promenade led by the Band of the RAF Regiment with the Queen's Colour of the RAF Regiment uncased. The Freedom Scroll was accepted by Air Vice Marshal B C Yarde CVO, CBE, Commandant General of the RAF Regiment and Inspector of Ground Training, on behalf of the Squadron and the RAF. The Squadron Commander, Squadron Leader A R Poole DSO, DFC, in return, presented the Mayor of Southport, Councillor F E Thornley, with a silver rose bowl from the Squadron at the Freedom Ball held in the Manchester Road Territorial Army Barracks in the evening. The ceremony on the promenade saw a fly-past of four Meteor F8s from No 611 Squadron, now based at Hooton Park.

End of the Auxiliaries

Unfortunately, due to further economic cuts and the infamous Defence Review of 1957 by Duncan Sandys, No 2611 Squadron was notified in January 1957 that it was shortly to disband and finally passed into the history books on 10 March 1957 having enjoyed the Freedom of Entry into Southport for only seven months. The value of these squadrons has since been realised and in 1979 the first four airfield defence squadrons were re-activated and several served in the Gulf during the 1990-91 Gulf War. The economic cuts did not stop with 2611 Squadron as the whole of the Royal Auxiliary Air Force was disbanded together with No 982 Signals Unit at Woodvale and Nos 610 and 611 Squadrons at Hooton Park along with all other auxiliary units. All units disbanded on 10 March 1957 and Hooton Park and many other airfields closed for ever as military airfields.

Much of early 1957 was taken up with the preparations for the SSAFA Air Display which was to take place on 10 June. It partly celebrated the demise of the Spitfire PR19s and hailed the Mosquito TT35s to the THUM Flight and was to be the last large RAF public air display ever to be seen at Woodvale, another shade of economic cuts. The display has already been mentioned and was marred by two of the Fleet Air Arm Sea

The last three Spitfires in routine RAF Service were retired on 12 June 1957 to be replaced with Mosquitoes TT35's in the Thum Flight. Last line up with the ground crew looking on with three pilots being left to right: Eric Richards and John Formby with a Short Bros. and Harland pilot brought in for the last flight on the Thum Flight was now down to three aircraft. Note replacement Mosquito in the background.

Final photo call for the ground crew who lovingly kept these Spitfires flying.

Two out of three taxi-ing to depart. Note that one would not start and had to be flown out the next day. The aircraft are PS853, PM631 and PS915 all of which are still flying with the RAF Battle of Britain Memorial Flight. Today at RAF Conningsby, Lincs.

PS853 took off but suffered engine failure and undertook a forced landing. It was almost stationary when a wheel dropped into a rabbit hole and tipped it on its nose. Damage was minimal and it was able to be repaired and flown out a few days later. These three aircraft were the embryo of the Battle of Britain Flight.
Stephenson Newspapers Ltd.

Hawks touching wings whilst in formation in cloud and resulted in them making a hasty landing, fortunately with no danger to life. Two months later, in September the Commanding Officer was warned of a possible IRA attack and extra guards were posted, again fortunately nothing materialised.

The void left by No 2611 Squadron and No 982 Signals Unit was filled on 1 January 1958 when No 5 Civilian Anti-Aircraft Co-Operation Unit (CAACU) flew in from Llanbedr, North Wales. In 1951 Spitfires had been withdrawn from all squadron service but some were still used to form units like the THUM Flight and CAACUs. Five of these units were formed during 1951 at Hornchurch, Little Snoring, Exeter, Llandow and Llanbedr, numbered 1 to 5 respectively. By 1954 the Spitfires and Beaufighters were replaced with either Mosquitoes, Vampires or Meteors. In the case of No 5 CAACU, Mosquito TT35s were delivered in 1954 closely followed by six Vampire Mk 5's in May and July of the same year. The Spitfire Mk 16's were phased out by the end of 1954. The first Meteor, an F4, arrived in December 1954 but was replaced by the first F8 in May 1955. More F8s arrived from Church Fenton on 4 May 1956 and the Vampires were allotted out by the end of that year. In November 1957 Home Command Admin Order No 24/57 authorised the re-deployment of No 5 CAACU from Short Bros and Harland, Llanbedr, to Short Bros and Harland, Woodvale. Four Meteors, three F8s and one T7 flew across on 20 December 1957 followed by two Mosquito TT35's on 13 January. the task of the unit was to provide targets for all three services on the Ty Croes Range, off the North Wales coast, together with requirements on other ranges, especially off Benbecula. Much of the job involved acting as targets for radar plotting in connection with simulated missile attacks but also involved anti-aircraft gun practice. The unit was kept very busy and sorties were flown virtually every day. The unit operated five Mosquitoes at Llanbedr but decided to take only one to Woodvale (VR806) with them, the others retiring to No 10 Maintenance Unit at Hullavington for storage and eventual scrap.

The Mosquito TT35s of the THUM Flight continued their daily climbs but their age was beginning to effect serviceability and the search was again underway for a replacement. With No 5 CAACU operating Meteors an F8, VZ508, was delivered from No 151 Squadron for dummy trials and whilst these were experimented upon for some time, the aircraft was turned down mainly due to lack of range, even with long range tanks. Another F8 was delivered from No 20 Maintenance Unit at Aston Down during early 1959 but research into shortening the climb had shown that the job could be done just as efficiently and cheaply by using radar tracked balloons. The very last THUM flight took place by a Mosquito TT35, TJ138, on 1 May 1959, the Mosquitoes passing to No 5 CAACU for a short while before moving to No 27 Maintenance Unit at Shawbury for scrapping although TJ138 managed to escape being kept as a museum aircraft. The two Meteor F8s were also passed to the CAACU and retained on strength. Due credit should be given to the air and ground crews that kept these aircraft maintained so that the climb could always take place. Bill Marshall was the senior engineer responsible and was with the Flight the whole time. It was his ingenuity and dedication, even though his health was none too good, that the THUM Flight achieved the records that it did.

The Mosquito completed the last of two thousand eight hundred sorties flown by the Flight with the loss of two Spitfires, two pilots but no Mosquitoes. One Mosquito was written off after a belly landing in October 1957 when Gordon Richards lost an engine in TK604 and could not lower his undercarriage. The aircraft landed on the cable drum suspended under the aircraft and slewed off the runway,

Photo collection of Thum Flight Mosquitoes.
Mosquito TA722 touching down on a bright summer day with the tented camp in the background, 1958.

TA641 parked by the control tower in the snow of winter 1958/9.

RS719 with accompanying 'Trolleyac' battery starter in front of the pair of hangars 1958.

TA722 still wearing yellow training bands on fuselage and wings. Parked outside the Maintenance Hangar (now RAF Hangar) by the main road in 1957.

TK604 outside the Brewery Lane Hangar in January 1958. This Mosquito suffered an engine failure and was written off in the resultant forced landing when only one wheel would come down. The pilot, Eric Richards, thought he had jettisoned the under fuselage winch on the beach but it hung up and he landed on it on the runway. It was stripped of engines and useful parts and burned with time expired Anson T21, VV324 at Woodvale on 8 January 1958.

Air Vice Marshall H.V. Slatterly AOC No. 64 Group RAF presenting Mr F. Chapman, Manager of Short Bros. & Harland Ltd., with one of the undamaged Spitfire propellor blades from PS853 after its forced landing in appreciation of the RAF's thanks for the work undertaken by the Thum Flight at the time of its disbandment. The blade is now on public view at the Southampton Hall of Aviation. Aircraft TJ138. *C.H. Loker via F. Chapman*

The very last Met flight by the Thum Flight with John Formby at the controls of TJ138 taking off for the last climb on 18 April 1959.
Visitor Series of Newspapers

John Formby receives the L.G. Groves Memorial Prize for services to the Met Office in 1958. He was also awarded the MBE in the same year. *John Formby*

fortunately not injuring the pilot. The aircraft was declared category E and written off being burned on the airfield with Anson T21, VV324, on 8 January 1958.

The Thum Flight had been operated for eight years by Short Bros and Harland Limited and since the death of Gordon Hargreaves in May 1952, led by John Formby, who in addition to the LG Groves Memorial Prize in 1958, was also awarded the MBE in the 1958 New Year's Honours List, possibly the only medal won at Woodvale. A gathering at Woodvale to mark the end of this truly epic Flight took place on 1 May attended by the Director General and other representatives of the Meteorological Office. John Formby flew

the last climb, including the now customary stop at Speke on the return and this was his one thousand two hundred and twenty seventh climb! He continued in the employment of Short Bros and flew Meteors with No 5 CAACU undertaking co-operation work at Fighter Control Units at Boulmer, Patrington, Bawdsey, Neatishead and Killard Point. He finally hung up his flying gloves in October 1959 having flown a total of 10,976 hours 25 minutes (equivalent to being airborne for a total of 457 days or 65 weeks, or one year seventeen weeks!) He flew 1,438 hours in Spitfire PR19s and 711 hours in Mosquito TT35s at Woodvale. If this is not a record it must be very close to one.

10 Air Experience Flight

The last unit to form at Woodvale was No 10 Air Experience Flight (AEF) which formed on 25 August 1958 with thirteen others around the UK. Flight Lieutenant F A Chapman AFM, RAFVR acted as Commanding Officer and was simultaneously Manager of Short Bros & Harland at Woodvale. The Flights were formed to give Air Training Corps and Combined Cadets Force cadets flying experience as part of their cadet training and to allow them to experience flying putting into practice the theory they learned with their units and determine whether they would like to try to become RAF aircrew later. The Flight at Woodvale has always operated five Chipmunk T10 aircraft and with the exception of the Commanding Officer, is manned by part time ex-RAF pilots now serving with the RAFVR(T) branch. The Flight has changed little in it's thirty three years of operation except a change of buildings and the inevitable change in aircraft. Cadets are drawn from Lancashire, Merseyside, Cheshire and Greater Manchester areas. An average of four thousand cadets are flown each year, the majority at weekends and approximately two thousand hours achieved. Occasionally the aircraft are flown to Valley for the weekend to give flying experience to cadets in North Wales. During Easter and Summer camps the aircraft are flown to RAF stations accommodating cadets in order to provide additional flying facilities there. The Flight has never lost an aircraft or life and when the University Air Squadrons re-equipped with Bulldogs, the RAF sold the older Chipmunks and refurbished the remainder and issued them to the AEFs and Elementary Flying Training Squadron and they have an unlimited life ahead of them. In fact during mid 1991 the aircraft have been completely changed again.

Squadron Leader Norman E Rose, AFC & Bar, AMN, RAF(Retd) was CO of 10 AEF from 1979 to 1984 and continued as a VR(T) pilot until he was 65-culminating in 47 years continuous service as an active military pilot flying RAF aircraft – a record in the Guinness Book of Records under Personal Aviation Records.

Two MBE's have been awarded to pilots from 10 AEF, Flight Lieutenants Harry Knight and James Reid for their services to the RAF each having served almost 30 years at Woodvale.

On 2 October 1983 RAF Woodvale flew the 1,000,000th cadet in the Air Experience Scheme in a Chipmunk of No 10 AEF. He was Cadet Warrant Officer Terry Jones from No 281 (Southport) Squadron and was flown by Flight Lieutenant Bill Orrell RAFVR(T), another long serving pilot with the Flight. Currently No 10 AEF has flown in the region of 150,000 cadets without incident, let alone any form of accident – this in itself must be some form of record. It must be a tribute to the dedication and superb engineering on the part of the ground crews and also to the flying skills of the part-time pilots of the RAFVR(T) with No 10 AEF.

There is an MP flying with 10 AEF, since 1985 – Mr Keith Mans. Also many famous war-time pilots have flown with the Flight. For example the pilot who assisted with dropping Douglas Baders' wooden leg after he baled out and was captured near St Omer in Northern France. This was Flight Lieutenant Harry Knight. Another was Wing Commander David Penman, DSO, OBE, AFC, who led the second wave of Lancasters on the Augsburg raid when Nettleton won his VC. Flight Lieutenant Bob Davies was also a war-time Lancaster pilot.

Several new Provost T1s were allotted to No 5 CAACU in May 1958 with the pilots converting and sharing them with the University Air Squadrons for a very short time. After about two months they were moved on. The summer of 1958 saw the Boy Entrants from St Athan and Cosford following the Halton Apprentices for the last year of the camps. Southampton University Air Squadron brought it's Chipmunks for a month long camp and the circuit was busy with Mosquitoes of the THUM Flight, the Meteors of No 5 CAACU in addition to the Anson communications aircraft belonging to the Station Flight. No 64 Group disbanded on 28 November 1958 and control of the THUM Flight and No 5 CAACU passed to No 12 Group, Fighter Command whilst the control of the University Air Squadrons and AEF were vested in Headquarters No 23 Group, Flying Training Command. At the same time Woodvale took over all the parenting responsibilities of RAF Fazakerley, Liverpool. Fazakerley had been a vast Balloon base during the war and the Reserve Centre for Liverpool thereafter. Now that the Royal Auxiliary Air Force had been disbanded there was no further use and upon closure its responsibilities passed to Woodvale. Two of its units, the Mobile Glider Servicing Party and the Motor Transport Repair and Servicing Squadron moved to Woodvale

Chipmunk T10 WP929 of No. 10 Air Experience Flight. Taken October 1968
APF

A Percival Provost T1 operated by the Civilian Fighter Control Co-operation Unit and No. 5 CAACU at Woodvale.
Dave Vernon

Meteors of No. 5 CAACU
Meteor F8 WH453 outside the 'Meteor' Hangar circa 1970.   *APF*

Meteor F8 WK884/V. This aircraft came to Woodvale from Llanbedr in 1958.
Note original natural metal finish.

Action photo of a Meteor F8 taking off for co-operation work circa 1970. The
camouflage paint was applied to all F8's with the unit in the late 1960's.

F8 WH303/W on the airfield circa 1969.

VZ 493/0 parked in front of buildings then used by the Air Ministry Works
Dept. circa summer 1968.

discussed on 20 January 1959 when the Station Commander, Squadron Leader F A Chapman, AFM, attended a conference at Headquarters Flying Training Command regarding the proposal to run down the RAF personnel at Woodvale. As a result of this meeting an announcement was made in October that the RAF personnel were to be withdrawn and a civilian contract extended to take over the entire running of the station except for instructors and staff of the University Air Squadrons and AEF. Woodvale's parenting responsibilities were to be handed over to other stations on 16 November and the station passed over to Short Bros & Harland Ltd on 1 December 1959.

10 May 1959. Squadron Leader F. Chapman with a handful of hailstones. Note
Chipmunk and Meteor in the background.   *F. Chapman*

on 1 December, Fazakerley now being closed down and down-graded to Class B (inactive). Except for a handful of government buildings which remain, the whole of the site, including balloon hangars, was developed as a housing estate in the late 1960s.

Whilst the THUM Flight and CAACU were in Fighter Command, Flying Training Command took over the other units at Woodvale on 12 January 1959. More changes which were to further reduce the standing of RAF Woodvale were

The accounts were the responsibility of RAF Haydock, near St Helens and 30 November saw the last official day of the existence of RAF Woodvale, it now having lost its STATION identity.

All remaining SNCOs and airmen were moved to RAF Haydock, the domestic site cleared and the Communal Site declared redundant. The married quarters, domestic site and hirings became the responsibility of Haydock and the establishment of Haydock and the establishment of RAF Woodvale cancelled. There were, of course, many RAF personnel left running the UAS's and No 10 AEF but the THUM Flight had now disbanded and the CAACU was entirely civilian manned. The Officers' Mess on the Communal Site remained open until alternative accommodation could be found for the Officers and Cadets of the University Air Squadrons and a scheme was submitted to convert the now unused Station headquarters into an Officers' Mess, no SNCOs or Airmens Mess being required. The scheme was approved and within eighteen months the current Officers' Mess, just inside the main gate, had been completely refurbished and opened together with the addition of three new living blocks to the rear. With effect from 15 August 1959 the command of the station was vested in the Commanding Officer of Liverpool University Air Squadron and was continued on the basis that the senior officer in either UAS takes command.

On 16 January 1959 the Air Navigation and Trading Company of Squires Gate applied for a licence for an airline route from Blackpool to Woodvale and on to London; and another route Blackpool – Woodvale – Isle of Man, on three days per week. The aircraft proposed by the Company were Miles Marathons and de Havilland Drovers. These services were never started. Earlier Silver City Airways had operated a car ferry service on the route Birmingham – Woodvale – Belfast (Nutts Corner) during the summer months of 1955 and 1956 using Bristol 170s. A few of these trips were made but did not prove to be economically viable. On the inaugural flight two representatives of the Automobile Association were given free flights to the isle of Man but not been told that the aircraft was not returning to Woodvale and they would have to make their own way home! The Silver City operations were conducted from one of the ground crew huts in a corner of a hangar.

On 10 May 1959 rather different objects fell out of the sky in the form of hailstones. A sudden storm sent huge hailstones down covering a large area around Formby. The stones were so heavy that they made holes in the fabric covered wings of several Chipmunks which were parked outside. They came so rapidly that the ground crews did not have enough time to push the aircraft into the hangars and several aircraft were flying with patches in their wings for some time afterwards. Rumour at the time suggested that the ground crews were so busy getting their cars into the hangar to avoid the hail that the aircraft were neglected! A year before the hail the station was hit by lightning which struck one of the offices and made a hole in the roof and other damage but without injury.

The 1960's saw little of note at Woodvale with the longest period unbroken by change since it opened. In September 1964 a team of American Drag racing cars arrived in Britain and held their first festival of Drag racing out of the USA at Woodvale. They were the first dragsters to reach two hundred miles per hour in Britain, in a quarter of a mile from a standing start! A second Drag Festival was held on 3 October 1965 using the main runway. On 1 September 1963, No 23 Group Flying Training Command disbanded at RAF Dishforth, Yorks and the station was taken over by No 25 Group in the same Command at RAF White Waltham, Berks.

Manchester University Air Squadron lost an aircraft (WP968) on 22 December 1965 when it crashed onto Winter Hill in the Pennines, fortunately the aircraft hit the ground at a very shallow angle in low cloud and the crew of two were able to walk away, shaken but unhurt. The University Air Squadrons have suffered very few accidents, WP980 of Liverpool University received minor damage in a forced landing at St Athan in September 1958. In the late 1960's the future of No 5 CAACU appeared uncertain; Nos 1 and 2 had disbanded and Nos 3 and 4 had amalgamated at Exeter becoming No 3/4 CAACU. Woodvale's strength had dwindled to three Meteor F8s and a T7 supplemented occasionally by the TT20s now operating from Exeter. The Woodvale based aircraft had no target towing capability and if sleeve targets were required the TT20s would operate from Woodvale for the period required, often over weekends. At one time the unit almost disbanded and most of the aircraft were allotted away but it received a reprieve and settled at three F8s and one T7 for the remainder of its existence. In August 1970 the units flying hours dwindled to 6.25 hours but increased to 42.50 in September with most sorties over the Ty Croes Range, but included sorties to the Manorbier Range (via Brawdy), Stornaway and Benbecula. Occasionally the aircraft would detach to Benbecula and operate for a few days. The routine was brightened in May 1971 when an Air Training Corps cadet, Staff Cadet Humphries, was flown to Squires Gate from Ronaldsway in the Isle of Man in the Snaefell to Blackpool Tower top to top race; with the help of Mr David Parker and his Meteor T7. He completed the sixty one mile race in forty three minutes, fifty eight seconds but unfortunately was not fast enough to win his class. Mr Parker was the Manager of Airwork Services Ltd who had won the servicing and operating contract from Short Bros & Harland Ltd in April 1962. He was the first person to make a flying model aircraft powered by steam in 1967.

David Parker, Manager of Airwork Services Ltd., stands in front of a 5 CAACU Meteor F8 shortley before the disbandment of the unit in 1971.

Demise of No 5 CAACU

The Ty Croes Range closed in 1971 and the last sortie was flown by Mr Parker in Meteor F8 WH453 on 30 June 1971; the unit continued with flights and sorties including Benbecula, Chivenor, Wittering, Abingdon, Sydenham and several air displays as the Meteor was now becoming something of a museum piece. Two Meteor TT20's arrived in October 1970 as No 3/4 CAACU had disbanded, but the towing cables and winches were removed before the aircraft reached Woodvale. With the Ty Croes Range closed there was little further use for the CAACU and the newly reformed No 7 Squadron at RAF St Mawgan could easily handle the tasks with its longer range Canberras. No 5 CAACU officially disbanded on 30 June 1971 but it's aircraft lingered for several months. Meteor F8's were WH453, WF711 and VZ508 and these were delivered to RAF Kemble, Glos, on 13 October 1971. They were subsequently passed to Flight Refuelling at Tarrant Rushton where they were converted to pilotless drones for use off the North Wales missile ranges operating out of Llanbedr (the original home of No 5 CAACU). Two are now in little pieces on the bottom of the Irish Sea but as far as the author knows, WH453 may still be intact (June 1991). The T7, WF791, was delivered to Kemble on 27 October and after being held in storage was passed to the Brawdy Station Flight. After operating there for a short time it was surveyed and realised that it was in far better condition that the T7 in use by the RAF display team, the Vintage Pair. It was returned to Kemble for a complete overhaul and flew from the Central Flying School at RAF Leeming, Yorks with the Vampire of the Vintage Pair, delighting thousands with the nostalgic sound of the early centrifugal flow jet engine. Unfortunately the aircraft was lost in a tragic accident at Coventry, on 30 May 1988, when taking part in a flying display. It should be remembered that many air displays are graced with the appearance of one of the three Spitfire PR19's of the Battle of Britain memorial Flight at Coningsby. all are ex-THUM Flight aircraft from Woodvale.

The two Meteor TT20's met different fates: WM224 was flown to RAF Swanton Morley, Norfolk, for non-destructive airframe testing. After finishing its useful life there it was sold to a local farmer and eventually bought by the publican of the Kings Head at North Weald (a famous Battle of Britain airfield) near Epping, Essex where it stood for several years in the car park. The final TT20 (WD646) flew to RAF

Two visiting Meteor TT20's temporarily based at Woodvale in October 1968. Note overwing winches and cables for target towing. Their parent was No. 2/3 CAACU at Exeter. *APF*

Cosford on 10 December 1971 and stood as a guardian with No 2030 Squadron Air Training Corps at Sheldon, West Midlands. These TT20s were probably the last of their type (converted NF11s) to fly routine military anywhere in the world – another record for Woodvale.

The closure of No 5 CAACU left Woodvale devoid of jet aircraft for the first time for many years and essentially in the same state as it is today with Liverpool and Manchester University Air Squadrons and No 10 AEF. Airwork Ltd had some spare capacity and they won the contract from the Ministry of Defence to re-cover the wings of the RAF Chipmunk fleet. In fact Chipmunks from all three services were seen at Woodvale including the famous Army "Spitmunk" (a camouflaged Chipmunk). Here the wings were stripped of linen, checked for corrosion and new Irish linen fitted and shrunk into place with an application of dope. At any one time up to four Chipmunks belonging to the RAF Primary Flying School, University Air Squadrons, Air Experience Flights etc would be in the maintenance hangar in addition to the station's own aircraft.

During 1973 and 1974 the derelict buildings on the perimeter of the airfield, the dispersals, sandbagged revetments, Flight Offices, stores and sleeping accommodation, all erected during the war, were demolished. They were now totally in ruins with roofs missing from most and the occasional squatter was found in the corner of one with some protection left. The clearance scheme greatly enhanced

Meteor T7 WF791, long standing mount of No 5 CAACU seen in December 1968 after just receiving a new paint job in light grey. The aircraft went on to serve at RAF Brawdy and then The Vintage Pair but was lost at Coventry in 1988. *APF*

A small arms ammunition store on the airfield identified by the No. 52 awaiting demolition in January 1973. *APF*

Fox Moth G-ADJH belonging to Norman Giroux was based at Woodvale for a short time after the hangars at Hesketh Park Aerodrome, Southport were demolished in the late 1960's. This aircraft was employed for pleasure flights off Birkdale Sands at Southport. Photo June 1970   *APF*

the appearance of the airfield but included the two remaining blister hangars on the railway side of the airfield. The Southport Aero Club had been using one and they were now allowed to use the empty hangar on the south side of the airfield unoccupied since the disbandment of No 2611 Squadron in 1957. This had been used for some aircraft respraying and the storage of the Piston Provosts.

From 1958 a detachment of No 281 (Southport) Squadron Air Training Corps had been using the buildings adjacent to this hangar. An ATC Squadron existed in Formby during the War but it closed shortly after. Flight Lieutenant Sid Brownlie formed a Detached Flight of the Southport Squadron with Flying Officer Colin Abrams. By 1960 the Flight had reached the required status to become a Squadron (over thirty enroled cadets) and was presented with its Warrant and new number, 1430 (Formby) Squadron. The ceremony was held at Holy Trinity Church, Rosemary Lane and the author was one of the standard bearers.

Civil Flying

Although Southport Aero Club was denied the use of the hangar and buildings, the Squadron moved across the airfield to the main site in 1967 occupying the old armoury, now not required by the RAF. The Squadron has since grown considerably in strength and today boasts many cadets, both male and female, an indoor rifle range, had a sailing dingy for many years operated by the Commanding Officer Alan McLellan, and excellent training facilities. With the rebuilding of the main buildings at Woodvale the Squadron lost its HQ and moved to two buildings previously occupied by 10 AEF. These buildings are very inferior to the original and split the Squadron's activities, especially in the Winter. The author was a cadet with the Squadron initially when located adjacent to the Brewery Lane hangar and moved with it across the airfield to the armoury building. He was subsequently commissioned in the RAFVR(T) and became adjutant of the Squadron for many years under the command of Flight Lieutenants John Hartley, Bob Williams and Alan McLellan. The Squadron rifle range opened in 1974 and is housed in the old Barrack Store, also on the main site. A Link Trainer was acquired by the Squadron and under the loving care of John Barton restored to full working condition. Unfortunately John became ill and subsequently died and there was no-one with his knowledge and dedication to continue with it.

Headlines in 1974 read "Concorde Crashes at Woodvale" and raised many eyebrows to say the least. However, it was only a model one, albeit costing £1,000 and taking four hundred and sixty hours to build. It happened at the National Model Aero Championship in August, now held annually at Woodvale. The Concorde suffered engine failure and crashed missing all the five thousand spectators. Knowing it could not be brought down safely it was allowed to crash in front of the crowd line.

After many years of trials and financial exercises, the RAF eventually decided to re-equip its University Air Squadrons with the Scottish Aviation Bulldog two seat trainer, starting in 1973. The RAF received the first production aircraft into its Flying Training Schools and the Central Flying School, and Manchester University Air Squadron received its first,

Woodvale from the air in 1970. The pair of hangars still stands as do the gun butts beyond the MT section. Half the MT section has already been demolished due to gale damage but the WT mast has not yet been relocated to the Main Site. The Station Workshops are also still standing. All buildings are white – not yet toned down. *APF*

Bulldog TI XX549 was delivered as the first to Woodvale on 17 May 1973 flown in by the CFI of Manchester UAS Flight Lieutenant Trevor W. Jackson.
Visitor Series of Newspapers

Squadron grouping around a Manchester UAS Bulldog in July 1974, left to right: Flight Lieutenant Mike Kirk, Flight Lieutenant Trevor W. Jackson, Flight Lieutenant Rod Newman, Flight Lieutenant Steve Fisher, ? , Squadron Leader Richard Gowring, Officer Commanding Manchester UAS. *APF*

XX549, on 17 May 1974 when Flight Lieutenant T W Jackson flew it in from RAF Little Rissington. It was soon followed by four more and the Squadron lost its Chipmunks immediately afterwards. Conversion under Squadron Leader David Fradley and later Squadron Leader Richard Gowring took little time and all cadets were converted in a few months.

In order to satisfactorily accommodate the Bulldogs a concrete hardstanding was required. The Bellman hangar of the pair nearest to the airfield on the Main Site required a considerable amount of expense to bring it to an acceptable standard and finance was not available. A very unfortunate decision was reached that it should be demolished and its base used as a hard standing, instead of both refurbishing it and providing a hardstanding. Accordingly it was demolished in 1974 and has been constantly missed ever since. At the same time Liverpool Squadron's Headquarters was refurbished, adjacent to the newly created hardstanding. Liverpool University Air Squadron received their first two Bulldogs on 16 May 1975 followed by the remaining two on 13 June 1975. At the same time the Chipmunk T10s of No 10 AEF were withdrawn and replaced with aircraft which had been totally

The original of the pair of Bellman Hangars on Main Site being demolished in October 1974. Its concrete base is the hardstanding for the civilian flying clubs.

Bulldog XX618/A of Yorkshire UAS after crashing onto Ainsdale Beach on 22 July 1976 whilst on summer camp at Woodvale. The aircraft failed to recover from a spin and the crew abandoned it over the beach.
Visitor Series of Newspapers

Bulldog XX630/A of LUAS after Flight Lieutenant 'Paddy' Cooney's successful forced landing. *Crown Copyright RAF Coltishall*

The Goodyear Airship 'Europe' landing at Woodvale in June 1976.
Visitor Series of Newspapers

refurbished; their new colour scheme matching those of the Bulldogs.

Bulldog flying suffered a double blow in July 1976 when two aircraft crashed onto the beach at Ainsdale, fortunately no-one was killed and neither belonged to a unit from Woodvale. The Commanding Officer of Yorkshire University Air Squadron, an ex-Manchester UAS instructor, Squadron Leader

George Dunn and his pupil baled out when they failed to recover from a spin. Squadron Leader Dunn landed just as his parachute fully deployed making a very heavy landing and injured his back. The aircraft crashed onto the sand and was a total wreck. Another Bulldog crew watched the accident and landed on the sand to render immediate assistance. Unfortunately, it hit some soft sand just as it was coming to a standstill and was flipped onto its back, writing it off. Manchester University Air Squadron almost suffered an accident when Flight Lieutenant Rod Newman was forced to execute a forced landing into some bushes just within the airfield boundary, due to engine failure. Fortunately, after a perfect landing no-one was hurt and the aircraft suffered no damage.

Another close-shave with a happy ending occurred to Flight Lieutenant "Paddy" Cooney of Liverpool University Air Squadron whilst at Summer camp at RAF West Raynham in August 1988. He suffered engine failure in Bulldog XX630 whilst formation flying at 500 ft and undertook a forced landing on the beach at Pakefield near Lowestoft. The aircraft stayed the right way up and although its wheels were almost covered by pebbles no damage was done. It took a Sea King helicopter to remove it.

In June 1976 the Goodyear airship "Europa" used Woodvale as a base during a month long goodwill tour of the UK. A special portable mooring mast was erected near to the control tower and the airship gave short flights from Woodvale to the Goodyear Company's guests and went on aerial tours of the North Wests' towns and cities. It was one hundred and ninety two feet long and fifty nine feet high with a fifty feet girth and gave cause for concern to the local police as motorists were distracted by it as they drove past the airfield.

In 1977 the national firemans strike brought "Green Goddess'– fire engines to Woodvale as the regular fire stations could not be used. Forty soldiers of 3rd Battalion, Queen's Regiment lived at Woodvale under the command of Regimental Sergeant Major Marshall providing men on two twelve hour shifts manning two machines. The arrival put some pressure on the Squadrons with both operating out of Liverpool's Headquarters for a while allowing the temporary firemen to set up an operations room in Manchester's building. The team covered the Formby and Southport area during October and November but were able to pull out with their twenty year old "Goddesses" once the strike was over.

Red Arrows

The 1970s have seen many visits by the Red Arrows on press days and also when operating for the Southport Flower Show each August. Many visiting movements are logged, especially service helicopters en route to Northern Ireland as Woodvale provided the perfect refuelling base before crossing the Irish Sea. The nearest RAF Airfields are Valley on Anglesey or Shawbury, Shropshire, both being fifty miles away. Several model aircraft championships have been held at Woodvale culminating in 1978 with the World Championship with entrants from all over the world, including Communist Countries attending. The event was marred by almost continual rain which washed out the week long event but did not stop it.

The Southport Aero Club was formed in 1951 but did not start flying until 1954 when it began operations off Southport Beach (Hesketh Park Aerodrome) utilising the World War One hangar occupied since before World War Two by Mr Giroux. The Club operated a Tiger Moth (G-ANOD) and a Foster Wikner Wicko (G-AFJB) off the sand for many years under the leadership of Dave Vernon, Cliff Jessop and Wilf Bold, with John Formby of Short Bros and Harland Ltd acting as Chief Instructor. The Club closed down for approximately two years in 1959 and reformed at Woodvale utilising the blister hangar which had just been vacated by No 186 Gliding School. Initially the Club had approximately twenty five members and flew an Aircoupe (G-ARHC). No proper club house accommodation existed and they originally

The Bellman Hangar by Brewery Lane on the south side of the airfield suffered years of neglect and was abandoned by the flying clubs in 1988/9 when the 'Meteor' hangar was vacated by the RAF and let to the civil clubs. This hangar was demolished in December 1988 but the buildings adjacent constructed for No. 2611 Squadron, RAF Regiment and later 1430 (Formby) Squadron ATC, remain. *APF*

The Red Arrows, the RAF's official aerobatic team opening their display at Woodvale in April 1973. Note that they were flying Hawker Siddeley Gnat Aircraft at the time.
Stephenson Newspapers

operated out of cars as the building on the west side of the airfield were too derelict to use or make economic repair. The ATC Squadron Headquarters moved across the airfield to the Main Site in 1967 and after a period lying empty, the three buildings originally constructed for No 2611 Squadron were handed over to the Southport Aero Club, although they were restricted to the Blister hangar. A second Forney Aircoupe (G-

Cessna 172 G-AVIR of West Lancs Aero Club in February 1980   *APF*

Cessna 150 G-AWXU of West Lancs Aero Club being re-fuelled near the MT Section in June 1970. The author undertook his first solo flight in this aircraft and it still serves with the club in 1991.   *APF*

Piper Cherokee G-AVPF of Woodvale Aviation Co. Ltd., photographed on 8 March 1991.   *APF*

Cherokee G-OWVA also operated by Woodvale Aviation Co. Ltd., photographed in March 1991   *APF*

ARHA) was added to the fleet plus a privately owned Cessna 172 (G-ARMP). This aircraft was later purchased by the Club and replaced a private Beagle Terrier (G-ASMZ). As the Bellman hangar was of no further use to the RAF it was leased to the Club and they moved across vacating the Blister hangar. The Aircoupes were then replaced by a Piper Colt (G-ARST) and Cessna (G-ATNZ) in addition to G-ARMP. The Colt was sold in 1966 and the Club left Woodvale and operated from Speke Airport from 1968.

After a period of about twelve months Stan Livesey and Cliff Jessop formed the West Lancs Aero Club at Woodvale with one aircraft, a leased Rollason Condor using a room in the guardroom as an office. Soon a Piper Cherokee was leased from Blackpool as the membership rose and eventually a Piper Colt (G-ARND) was purchased to replace the Cherokee. The Club expanded and moved into a caravan behind Station Headquarters eventually moving into the ROC Room in the end of the ejector seat bay. the Condor was replaced by a Tripacer (G-APWR) which in turn was sold and replaced by a Cessna 172 (G-AVIR).

At the demise of the Meteors of No 5 CAACU the Club was able to take over the whole of the Ejector Seat bay and its most dramatic growth commenced. The Colt and 172 were joined by a Cessna 150 (G-AXBU) then by Cessna 150 Aerobat (G-BCVH), then Grumman AA-IB (G-BCIL) and then by a further 150 (G-AVPH) making a total fleet of six aircraft. G-BCIL was replaced by a Cessna 172 (G-AVKG) and a seventh aircraft acquired in October 1978 when Beagle 206 (G-ATYW) was purchased for charter work, unfortunately this was not unsuccessful and it was subsequently sold. During 1979 the Colt (G-ARND) was sold. During July 1977 the Air Experience Flight moved from its original building in the old Link Trainer building to the old Works Office now vacated by Property Services Agency and acquired a new additional

Cessna 172 G-BHMI of West Lancs Aero Club in March 1991   *APF*

Cessna 150 G-BLVS of Wset Lancs Aero Club on a damp, dull March day in 1991.   *APF*

building purpose built. West Lancs Aero Club took over the old building and have recently undertaken large scale improvements including putting in new toilets and lowering the very high sill level of the windows, incorporating a simulator room and lecture and private study rooms. The Club now operates with six full time instructors and operates seven days a week subject to weather conditions. The Club has integrated with the service flying at Woodvale and utilises Air Traffic Control when open but operates its own crash vehicle outside station open hours. It's fleet in 1991 comprises Cessna 150s G-BAXU, BEHW, BLVS and GFLY; 172 G-BHMI and Warriors G-BNNO and BOTN.

A second club was formed after the West Lancs Aero Club, in March 1969, named the Woodvale Aero Club and is now known as the Woodvale Aviation Company Ltd. It originally operated from the buildings on the south side of the airfield vacated by the Southport Aero Club and operated a Cherokee G-AVFP and Cessna 150 G-AWXU followed by an Emeraude G-ARUV later joined by John Moore Jnr's Cherokee Six. Initially the club undertook PPL training and touring but reformed and renamed under Ian McConnochie it moved to portacabins adjacent to the Meteor hangar on Main Site in October 1988 whilst waiting for the Liverpool University Air Squadron's building to become available and where it has operated from since May 1990. This company specialises in instructors courses, Basic Commercial Pilots Licence (BCPL), Instrument Meteorology Conditions Rating (IMC), Instrument Rating (IR) and Twin Ratings with the emphasis on professional training. The Company also operates an Islander based at Manchester Airport for Datapost charter work and undertakes engine, airframe and instrument

PM631 in D-Day markings standing outside its home of 30 years ago at the Thum Flight Reunion in June 1987.   *APF*

maintenance and mods for Annual Inspections. The Fleet of Woodvale Aviation Co Ltd as at 1991 comprises three PA-28 140 Cherokees G-AVFP, BBLA and OWVA; PA-28 161 Warrior G-OANC; Chipmunk G-BCDC (ex WD388) and Aztec G-AXAX.

The Royal Observer Corps have always had a presence at Woodvale, initially operating from a building adjacent to the railway, moving across to the Guard Room and in the end of the Ejector Seat Bay. In the late 1960s it moved to its present Headquarters in a specially constructed underground building adjacent to the dual carriageway. The main role is not the logging of aircraft as in war-time days but the plotting of nuclear explosions and monitoring fallout with associated work in the event of nuclear attack. Although a smaller risk now threatens NATO and the British Isles the ROC still undertakes a very important civil defence role and is manned entirely by volunteers who give up a considerable amount of free time to train.

To celebrate the 30th Anniversary of the last Spitfire flight from Woodvale with the 'Thum Flight' a reunion was organised at Woodvale on 10 June 1987 – exactly 30 years to the day. Pilots and Support crew are shown here in front of PM631 (ex Thum Flight) specially flown in for the day by Squadron Leader Paul Day of the Battle of Britain Memorial Flight. Left to right standing: John Formby, Eric Richards, Brenda Youlton, Fred Chapman, John Wood, ?, George Shroud, ?, Ronnie Madden, ?. Kneeling: Dennis Thackery, Larry Rugland, Jerry Stern and ?.   *Crown Copyright – RAF Sealand*

Woodvale Today

Today Woodvale is but a shadow of it former self when it had two thousand personnel supporting three front line squadrons and numerous support squadrons and functions. It is one of the very few remaining "Temporary" airfields built for the duration of World War Two and now, fifty years afterwards it is still a very active RAF station playing a vital support role in todays much reduced streamlined RAF. With the exception of the Main Site, all its dispersed living and communal sites have been long since demolished with one or two building only remaining on the Sick Quarters and No 1 WAAF Sites. Of the four hangars that once graced the airfield only two are left, the ten blister hangars have also gone. The University Air Squadrons provide pre-service training to those students who have gained University Cadetships and are having their University tuition paid prior to joining the RAF upon graduation and undertaking the Officers Course at RAF Cranwell. Most are to be aircrew and will have attained a considerable number of hours prior to starting flying training on either Jet Provosts or Tucanos.

The benefit of Woodvale can be gauged by the recent Gulf War when Flt Lt John Peters, one of the pilots depicted on television with a battered and bruised face, undertook his training with Manchester and Salford Universities Air Squadron from 1981 to 1983. Another of many combat pilots trained at Woodvale was Flt Lt Keith Collister, originally from the Isle of Man who piloted the first RAF Jaguar which crashed, unfortunately costing him his life.

The University Air Squadrons also offer training to a limited number of undergraduates who are not committed to join the RAF. Prospective navigators, ground branch officers who have gained University Cadetships are members and are given air experience together with other instruction about leadership, the RAF, and other pre-entry subjects. Manchester and Salford Universities Air Squadron, as it was renamed in April 1975, has approximately forty eight pilots, and Liverpool thirty three, both including females, flying five and four Bulldog aircraft respectively. Each pilot flies approximately thirty three hours per year on a two year course, part at Woodvale during weekdays, Easter and Christmas Camps and partly at annual summer camp at a different RAF station. After two years the student can remain for a third year at the discretion of the Commanding Officer.

The other unit, No 10 Air Experience Flight, remains as before flying young ATC and CCF cadets, now both male and female, and is responsible for giving air experience flying to hundreds of cadets every year and no doubt gives many young people their first taste of flying (including the author) and gives them experience of the freedom and thrill of flying, and helps them decide whether the RAF could be a career for them. No 10 AEF moved to their new building at the end of 1990 on the site of the old Station Armoury, used for many years by the resident ATC Squadron, No 1430 Squadron (now 611 Squadron).

Also at Woodvale are the HQ of No 611 Squadron, Air Training Corps, which is the renumbered 1430 Squadron. It was renumbered when No 611 (West Lancs) Royal Auxiliary Air Force Squadron Association formed and "Adopted" the Squadron at a service on 21 November 1987. The Squadron

Bulldog T1 XX668/1 of Manchester & Salford University Air Squadron in the refurbished hangar in March 1991   *APF*

Bulldog T1 XX686/U of Liverpool University Air Squadron taxi-ing out from the old RAF dispersal – once the floor of No. 1 Bellman hangar – in June 1987. *APF*

During 1990 the Bulldog Fleet was refurbished and upgraded with the addition of strobe lights, the installation of VOR, DME and ILS plus a transponder. Here the new lights and aerials can be seen, March 1991. *APF*

With the Services now offering equal opportunities (almost) for women the UAS's are accepting women for pilot training whilst at University. Here is Cadet Pilot Sharon Banks with Cadet Pilot Adam Sullivan of MASUAS in June 1991. *APF*

The view of the main gate at RAF Woodvale as seen today. The guardroom is on the right with the Officers' Mess behind. In front of the Mess is gate guardian Meteor T7 WA591. *APF*

Chipmunk T10 WP900/15 of No. 10 AEF June 1987. *APF*

operates out of the old PSA building near the MT Section and another temporary building put up for No 10 AEF before it moved to its present location (see map). No 611 Squadron also uses a room in the Headquarters of Merseyside Wing, Air Training Corps which moved from RAF Sealand to Woodvale and occupies a purpose built building also near to the MT Section.

1990 and 1991 has seen great changes at Woodvale. In an attempt to contain rapidly rising costs and a diminishing defence budget one runway (17/35) was put onto a non maintenance basis in 1985 and plans made to sell off parts of the airfield and a possible supermarket built adjacent to the coast road at the northern edge of the airfield. The encroachment of housing and lack of understanding of people who moved into the area fully aware that an airfield has existed at Woodvale for fifty years, and now complain about noise, caused a re-think and the runway was reopened to keep noise to a minimum and also raise safely margins. However, some of the land to the Formby end of the airfield has been made available to the Army as it is not needed for RAF operations but, fortunately cannot be developed. The main runway has been resurfaced and all other operating surfaces are subject to planned maintenance.

Several of the buildings on the Main Site have been rebuilt with new Headquarters for the two University Air Squadrons and No 10 Air Experience Flight, the hangar totally

Woodvale Ground Crew June 1991, left to right: Ron Charnock, Geo. Yates, Ian Longstaff, Al Taylor, Nigel Furlong, Gordon Humphries, Phil Davidson (rear), John Cooper, Peter Thompson, Squadron Leader R. Newman (MASUAS), Cadet Pilots Sharon Banks and Adam Sullivan (MASUAS).

re-clad and refurbished, the building of a new hardstanding for all aircraft and the concentration of the RAF element into one specific part of Woodvale. The other hangar has been handed over to West Lancs Aero Club and Woodvale Aviation Co Ltd and they also enjoy full use of their buildings and the airfield. Woodvale is a true "Joint User" operating both RAF and civil aircraft but remaining firmly in RAF control although the civilian operating contract comes up for renewal every three years. CSE Ltd lost the contract in April 1991 to Serco Ltd; the Chipmunk fleet of five aircraft was replaced with refurbished aircraft with VHF radios in June 1991 and the Bulldog fleet has been updated. This comprises the installation of VOR, DME and ILS together with a transponder and strobe lights greatly enhancing the training capacity of these aircraft as well as safety.

As far as can be seen at the time of writing, there is little likelihood of change at RAF Woodvale. Demand for pilots for the RAF remains and the preparation of future RAF personnel and awareness of the RAF are offered by the resident units. Woodvale is the only RAF station in the North West of England and there are no more flying stations until one reaches Macrihanish off the Western Highlands of Scotland. Rumours of closure have been heard continuously since 1946 but it has thwarted all the critics, anti-noise lobby, CND, and pacifists and, hopefully, will still be here to celebrate its one hundredth birthday. Woodvale was designed and built to protect the people of Merseyside and North West England and was home to several thousand airmen and airwomen over fifty years. It is known only to a few in the UK but forgotten by none − long may it stay in RAF colours and never may it be forgotten.

COMMANDING OFFICERS

Flight Lieutenant R A Marwick	25 October 1941	19 December 1941	
Wing Commander G D Pinkerton DFC	19 December 1941	15 January 1942	
Group Captain J A McDonald CBE, AFC	15 January 1942	14 October 1942	
Wing Commander T N Hayes DFC	14 October 1942	25 October 1942	
Group Captain V S Bowling	25 October 1942	16 February 1943	
Wing Commander E R Isherwood DFC, AFC	16 February 1943	28 March 1943	
Wing Commander S G Beaumont MBE	28 March 1943	6 April 1943	
Group Captain V S Bowling	6 April 1943	26 August 1943	
Group Captain T B Prickman OBE	26 August 1943	22 September 1943	
Group Captain C Walter OBE	22 September 1943	15 August 1944	
Wing Commander E P Gibbs DFC	15 August 1944	18 August 1944	
Wing Commander J W Rayner	18 August 1944	14 August 1944	
Wing Commander C R Strudwick	24 August 1944	7 April 1945	
Commander Fussell, RN	7 April 1945	22 February 1946	
Wing Commander R C Reade MBE	22 February 1946	19 June 1946	
Squadron Leader W J Leather DFC	19 June 1946	5 November 1947	OC 611 Sqn
Flight Lieutenant F L Dent	5 November 1947	1 September 1948	
Flight Lieutenant F J Neale	1 September 1048	4 September 1948	
Flight Lieutenant Oldfield	4 September 1948	24 September 1948	
Flight Lieutenant H K Snell	24 September 1948	16 October 1948	
Squadron Leader R P Beamont DSO, DFC	1 September 1948	5 January 1949	OC 611 sqn
Squadron Leader W E V Mallins DFC	5 January 1949	20 June 1949	
Squadron Leader C G Reeves MBE	20 June 1949	11 September 1951	
Squadron Leader D W Baldwin	11 September 1951	4 February 1954	
Squadron Leader E D Griffiths	4 February 1954	21 October 1956	
Squadron Leader F Ellison OBE, AFC	18 June 1956	21 October 1957	
Squadron Leader F R Chapman AFM	21 October 1957	8 March 1960	
Squadron Leader N G Jones	8 March 1960	1 October 1962	OC LUAS
Squadron Leader R B Gubbins	1 October 1962	29 September 1963	OC LUAS
Squadron Leader F D G Clark BA	29 September 1963	12 September 1966	OC LUAS
Squadron Leader D J House	12 September 1966	2 March 1968	OC MUAS
Squadron Leader H G Boyne	2 March 1968	29 March 1971	OC LUAS
Squadron Leader A Withington	29 March 1971	31 July 1974	OC LUAS
Squadron Leader R J Gowring	31 July 1974	22 October 1976	OC MUAS
Squadron Leader R A Redmore	22 October 1976	10 December 1976	OC LUAS
Squadron Leader M L Schofield	10 December 1976	17 March 1979	OC MASUAS
Squadron Leader P R Jeffers	17 March 1979	29 October 1979	OC LUAS
Squadron Leader F C R Dicks	29 October 1979	18 January 1982	OC MASUAS
Squadron Leader G Timms	18 January 1982	24 May 1985	OC MUAS
Squadron Leader M B Connell	24 May 1985	12 October 1987	OC MASUAS
Squadron Leader K Lawry	12 October 1987	8 May 1988	OC LUAS
Squadron Leader C Wright	8 May 1988	Present	OC MASUAS

Squadron Leader F.D.G. Clark BA handing over command of the station to Squadron Leader D.J. House (right) on 12 September 1966.

Squadron Leader H.G. Boyne (left) seen in front of a LUAS Chipmunk handing control over to Squadron Leader Alan Withington on 29 March 1971.

Squadron Leader F.D.G. Clark BA (left) taking over command from Squadron Leader R.B. Gubbins on 29 September 1963. Both Squadron Leaders were also Commanding Officers of Liverpool UAS.

Squadron Leader D.J. House (left) handing command of RAF Woodvale over to Squadron Leader H.G. Boyne (right) 2 March 1968.

Squadron Leader Richard Gowring (seated) takes over command from Squadron Leader Alan Withington on 31 July 1974.   *APF*

UNITS BASED AT RAF WOODVALE

UNIT		IN	FROM	OUT		TYPE(S)
No 308	Squadron	12 Dec 41	Northolt	2 Apl 42	Exeter	Spitfire II Spitfire Vb
No 835	Defence Sqn	Dec 41	Formed	11 Feb 42	Renumbered No 2835 Defence Sqn	None
No 2835	Defence Sqn	11 Feb 42	Renumbered	10 Oct 42	Zeals	None
No 315	Squadron	2 Apl 42	Northolt	5 Sep 42	Northolt	Spitfire Vb
No 285	Squadron Detachment	14 Apl 42	Wrexham (HQ)	27 Aug 43	HQ moved from Honiley	Oxford I/II Defiant TT
No 776	Squadron, FAA Detachment	16 May 42	Speke (HQ)	7 Apl 45	HQ moved in from Speke	Roc, Skua, Martinet, Chesapeake, Seafire
No 256	Squadron	4 Jun 42	Squires Gate	23 Apl 43	Ford	Defiant I, Beaufighter If & VIf, Blenheim
No 317	Squadron Detachment at Valley	5 Sep 42	Northolt	13 Feb 43	Kirton-in-Lindsay	Spitfire Vb
No 116	Squadron "C" flight	16 Nov 42	Speke	10 Sep 43	Digby	Oxford I/II
No 195	Squadron	9 Feb 43	Hutton Cranswick	13 May 43	Ludham	Hurricane I, Tiger Moth Typhoon IA/AB
No 198	Squadron	14 May 43	Manston	5 Jun 43	Martlesham Heath	Typhoon IA/IB
No 501	Squadron	5 May 43	Martlesham Heath	Jun 43	Westhampnett	Spitfire Vb
No 322	Squadron	12 Jun 43	Reformed from No 167 Squadron	30 Dec 43	Hawkinge	Spitfire Vb
No 9	Group Communications Flight	5 Aug 43	Salmesbury	26 Aug 43	Salmesbury	Cleveland, Leopard Moth, Master III, Oxford, Dominie, Mentor, Vega Gull
No 256	Squadron Detachment at Malta	25 Aug 43	Ford	25 Sep 43	en route Malta	Mosquito XII
No 285	Squadron	27 Aug 43	Honiley	19 Nov 44	Andover	Defiant TTI, Martinet, Oxford, Hurricane II, Beaufighter I
No 222	Squadron	30 Dec 43	Hornchurch	14 Feb 44	Catterick en route Acklington	Spitfire XI
No 9	Group AA School	Jan 44	Speke	Aug 44	Disbanded	None
No 12	(Pilot) Advanced Flying Unit	10 Jan 44	Grantham	7 Feb 44	Poulton	Blenheim V
No 219	Squadron	11 Feb 44	Acklington	28 Apl 44	Honiley	Mosquito NF.XVII
No 316	Squadron	16 Feb 44	North Africa	28 Apl 44	Coltishall	Spitfire Vb, Mustang III
No 12	(Pilot) Advanced Flying Unit	21 Mar 44	Poulton	16 Aug 44	Spitalgate (Grantham)	Blenheim V
No 63	Squadron Detachments at Ballyhalbert and Dundonald	27 Apl 44	Turnhouse	28 May 44	Lee-on-Solent	Hurricane, Spitfire Vb
No 650	Squadron "B" Flight	18 May 44	Cark (HQ)	26 May 44	Flight Disbanded	Martinet I, Spitfire, Hurricane IIC & IV, Master
No 63	Squadron	3 Jul 44	Lee-on-Solent	30 Aug 44	Lee-on-Solent	Spitfire Vb
No 577	Squadron	19 Nov 44	Lee-on-Solent	11 Oct 45	Barrow	Hurricane IV, Spitfire, Vengeance TT.IV, Oxford
No 776	Squadron FAA	7 Apl 45	Speke	6 Oct 45	Burscough	Skua, Chesapeake, Roc, Martinet TT.1, Defiant TT.III
No 889	Squadron FAA	1 Jun 45	Reformed	10 Aug 45	HMS Ravager	Hellcat I & II(PR)
No 736B	Squadron FAA	28 Jun 45	Hal Far (Malta)	20 Jul 45	Fearn	Seafire XV, Dominie I, Beaufighter X
No 816	Squadron FAA	1 Jul 45	Machrihanish	11 Aug 45	Inskip	Firefly NF.I
No 736B	Squadron FAA	17 Aug 45	Fearn	26 Sep 45	Disbanded	Seafire XV, Dominie I, Beaufighter X
No 889	Squadron FAA	28 Aug 45	Belfast	10 Sep 45	HMS Trouncer	Hellcat I & II(PR)

No 822	Squadron FAA	28 Aug 45	Belfast	4 Oct 45	Burscough	Barracuda II(ASR), Firefly FR.1
No 5	(Motor Transport) Company	22 Feb 46	Liverpool	15 Sep 46	Disbanded	None
No 611	(West Lancs) Squadron AuxAF	22 Jul 46	Hooton Park	10 Jul 51	Hooton Park	Spitfire XIV & F.22, Meteor F.4 & T7, Harvard
No 2	(Motor Transport) Company Detachment	15 Sep 46	Leicester East (HQ)	16 Nov 46	Warton	None
No 2611	(West Lancs) Light AA Squadron AAF Regiment	1 Oct 47	Formed	10 Mar 57	Disbanded	None
No 186	Gliding School	Dec 47	Hooton Park	Dec 51	Hawarden	Cadet I & III, Sedburgh
University of Liverpool Air Squadron		2 Jul 51	Hooton Park	To Date		Chipmunk T10 Bulldog T1
No 19	Reserve Flying School	13 Jul 51	Hooton Park	20 Jul 54	Disbanded	Chipmunk T10, Oxford I, Tiger Moth, Anson T21
THUM Flight		13 Jul 51	Hooton Park	1 May 59	Disbanded	Spitfire PR19 & F24, Mosquito TT35, Meteor F8
Civilian Fighter Control Co-operation Unit		54	Formed	May 56	Disbanded	Oxford I, Provost T1
Manchester University Air Squadron		14 Mar 53	Barton	Apl 75	Renamed MASUAS	Chipmunk T10, Bulldog T1
No 982	Signals Unit	May 55	Formed	1 Mar 57	Disbanded	None
Western Sector Flight		56	Squires Gate	25 Oct 57	Disbanded	Oxford I, Meteor F8 Anson C19 & T21
No 5	Civilian Anti-Aircraft Co-operation Unit	1 Jan 58	Llanbedr	30 Jun 71	Disbanded	Mosquito TT35, Anson T21, Meteor T7, F8 & TT20
No 10	Air Experience Flight	25 Aug 58	Formed	To Date		Chipmunk T10
Motor Transport Repair & Servicing Squadron		1 Dec 58	Fazakerley	? 59		None
Mobile Glider Servicing Party		1 Dec 58	Fazakerley	59	Shawbury	None
Manchester & Salford University Squadron		Apl 75	Renamed from MUAS	To Date		Bulldog T1

Accidents

21 December 41

Plt Off E Krawczynski (28) of 308 (Polish) Squadron killed when Spitfire Vb crashed and buried its nose deep into sand by Ribble estuary, buried at Our Lady's Church, Formby.

9 January 42

Sqn Ldr M J Wesolowski (28) of 308 (Polish) Squadron collided with Fg Off Dolicher in dawn flying accident. Wesolowski's aircraft entered spin and crashed killing him, Dolicher maintained control and landed safely. Spitfire Vb. Buried Our Lady's Church, Formby.

13 February 42

Fg Off Paley, of No 308 (Polish) Squadron, baled out of a Spitfire in mock dog fight after blacking out. Pilot OK, aircraft written off.

19 July 42

Sgt T T Nawrocki (28) of 315 (Polish) Squadron killed in Spitfire Vb, W3628, crashed at Lunecliffe, two miles South of Lancaster. Buried at Our Lady's Church, Formby.

28 August 42

Fg Off B J Sawiak (23) of 315 (Polish) Sqn, flying from Valley crashed after interception with Ju88 over Northern Ireland, near Ballyhalbert. Crashed near Dublin and died of wounds. Ju88 subsequently crashed in Southern Ireland. Spitfire Vb. Buried Our Lady's Church, Formby.

1 September 42

Defiant T3923 of 285 Squadron (Detachment) collided with motor roller whilst taxiing. Aircraft damaged, pilot OK.

31 October 42

Sqn Ldr R De W K Winlaw , Commanding Officer and Plt Off C T Ashton (Navigator) killed in Beaufighter 1f X7845 of 256 Squadron. Collided with a Wellington (BK234) in mid air near Bangor, North Wales, both aircraft crashed and all seven killed. Winlaw buried on 8 November location unknown, CO's ashes scattered over the sea.

28 December 42

Fg Off Pucek of 317 (Polish) squadron lost in a Spitfire in formation flying in cloud and failed to return. No trace found.

1 February 43

Spitfire Vb of No 317 (Polish) Squadron overturned on landing at Valley after brake pressure failure, pilot, Flying Officer Birtus unhurt.

7 February 43

Defiant I V1134 of 285 squadron (Detachment) struck ground on diving attack exercise at Plumley, Cheshire. Aircraft turned over and was completely destroyed. Pilot, Sgt W H Meakin unhurt.

9 February 43

Flt Lt D Toone and Plt Off W F Hutchings (navigator), both of No 256 Squadron reported missing 20 miles WNW of Squires Gate on a GCI. Beaufighter, no trace found.

18 February 43

Typhoon IB, EJ909 crashed close to airfield wrecking aircraft but pilot, Sgt Lindsay, OK.

9 March 43

Typhoon IB, DN474 crashed and written off. Pilot, Sgt Jones badly injured but survived.

10 March 43

Beaufighter of 256 Sqn crash landed on station sports field after one engine failed. Pilot Plt Off P Harrison-Yates was killed, navigator Sgt W Patterson survived with slight injuries. Engine failed 50 miles out to sea. Harrison-Yates' ashes scattered over Irish Sea from Beaufighter of his squadron.

9 April 43

Sgt W A Dixon (Canadian) (24) of 195 Squadron killed in Typhoon IB DN424 whilst taking off, crashing immediately over railway line, killed instantly. Buried St Peter's Church, Formby.

16 April 43

Plt Off Morgan of 195 Squadron crash landed at Warton in Typhoon IB just short of runway onto mud flats, aircraft salvaged, pilot OK.

7 May 43

Sgt Duckworth of 285 Squadron (Detachment), injured in crash landing in Oxford X7280 on Heavy AA co-operation exercise. Hit anti-landing post on landing. Badly injured, died 17 October 1943.

8 May 43

Sgt Burgess of 285 Squadron (Detachment) force-landed Defiant N1706 at Squires Gate after hitting flock of pigeons at Heysham on Light AA exercise. Treated for multiple cuts.

26 May 43

Pilot Officer Robert Ralph Walters, 144462, RAF (VR), (20). Typhoon of 198 Sqn. Hit sea one mile off-shore Lytham St Annes. Body found 5 June, buried 10 June. Son of Leonard Ralph and Anne Kathleen Walters of Matfield, Kent. Buried Lytham St Annes Park Cemetery.

6 June43

Oxford II R5974 of 116 Squadron, undercarriage collapsed whilst taxiing, pilot Flt Sgt S F Hetherington not hurt.

9 August 43

Oxford HM833 of 285 Squadron (Detachment) crash landed after pilot lost control. Pilot OK

20 August 43

Fg Off Flinterman unable to retract undercarriage in unknown aircraft, emergency landing and undercarriage collapsed, aircraft damaged but pilot OK.

24 August 43

Plt Off Van Bergan of 322 Squadron crash landed in Spitfire, pilot OK.

25 August 43

Flt Sgt Bolland of 285 Squadron (Detachment) in Martinet MS507 had engine failure just after take off and force-landed at Harrington Barracks, Formby. Aircraft burst into flames but pilot pulled clear by soldiers with little injury.

25 August 43

Spitfire of No 322 Squadron executed belly landing and overturned. Pilot unhurt.

23 September 43

Midshipman Bushby of 776 Squadron, FAA suffered engine failure in Chesapeake AL919 whilst drogue towing over the Ainsdale beach range and just had enough height to land with undercarriage retracted on grass at north end of airfield. Pilot OK.

30 September 43

Sub Lt Mogridge of 776 Squadron, FAA damaged the airscrew in Chesapeak AL950 whilst engaged in low level exercises over the sea, he just managed a wheels-up landing inside the airfield boundary. Pilot OK.

28 October 43

Spitfire of 322 Squadron force-landed near Preston with engine trouble. Pilot OK.

6 November 43

Spitfire of 322 Squadron crash landed on airfield, pilot OK.

15 November 43

Flt Sgt Burgess of 285 Squadron hit obstruction whilst taxiing Oxford I LX464 damaging both props.

29 November 43

Plt Off Smith and Flt Sgt A W Pointer of 285 Squadron undershot at night in Oxford LX462 with minor damage. No injuries to crew.

12 December 43

Blenheim AZ877 of "W" Detachment of No 12 (P)AFU executed a belly landing due to pilot error, no injuries to crew.

8 March 44

Skua of 776 Squadron, FAA, crashed into sea off Southport pier, pilot OK.

18 March 44

USAAF Lockheed P-38 Lightning from BAD No. 2 at Warton crashed on sand dunes due west of the airfield. Pilot, Lt H W Vallee killed.

21 March 44

Flt Sgt Kowalski of 316 (Polish) Squadron developed engine trouble and crashed in Spitfire LFVb in attempted forced landing. Pilot died from injuries, buried in Formby 25 March, location unknown.

14 April 44

Sqn Ldr G F Harris of 285 Squadron undershot in Oxford I LX642, little damage, pilot unhurt.

21 May 44

Fg Off G L Storey of 63 Squadron spun in steep turn in Spitfire and crashed into houses in Ainsdale. Aircraft burst into flames and killed pilot and injured two civilians attempting rescue.

25 June44

Blenheim I AZ884 of 12 (P)AFU landed with undercarriage up, pilot not hurt.

6 July 44

Blenheim V BA783 of 12 (P)AFU overshot on single engined approach and cartwheeled into ground from 100 feet. Instructor and pilot badly burned.

10 August 44

Blenheim of 12 (P)AFU crashed killing Sgt D L Edmunds and Flt Sgt J C Stone.

13 August 44

Blenheim BA104 of 12 (P)AFU belly landed, pilot OK.

25 October 44

B-24 Liberator of the 740th Bomb Squadron, 446th Bomb Group, Bungay crashed on landing in bad weather near 285 Squadron dispersal. Dragged wing on attempted landing and cartwheeled and blew up 20 on board. Four killed outright and three died in SSQ later, rest (13) seriously injured.

13 January 44

Blenheim V AZ877 of 12 (P)AFU belly landed, pilot OK.

13 February 45

Flt Lt Smith (pilot) of an unknown unit crashed in a Mosquito making single-engined approach. Fg Off Stevenson (nav) sustained fractured arm.

14 February 45

Mosquito of unknown unit crashed on emergency landing on one engine. Pilot, Sqn Ldr Cowper not injured.

4 May 45

WO Thomas Price of 577 Squadron (Detachment) killed in Hurricane LF652, crashed into sea off Southport pier.

31 July 47

Fg Off Robert Ivor Reid (No 91252) RAF (AuxAF) in Spitfire F21 LA211 of 602 Sqn on summer camp at Woodvale, crashed at 08.45 in sea off the Flyde coast off Rossall. Duty was air-to-air firing exercise. The aircraft was seen to circle after engine cut, lost height and dived into the sea - may have attempted a ditching. Engine trouble suspected but not confirmed and wreckage was not recovered. Low mist may have caused the pilot to misjudge his height above the sea. The pilot, a chartered accountant of Glasgow was buried at Thornton-Cleveleys Plot R2 Grave 798.

8 May 48

Spitfire XIVe RN210 of No 611 Squadron crashed on Freckleton Marsh near Grange Farm. Reported that the pilot Fg Off R H P Griffiths lost consciousness due to oxygen failure at 21,000 ft. Buried St Peter's Church, Formby.

3 July 48

Fg Off Geldart of No 611 Squadron lost control of Spitfire XIV NM814 on a cross country near Kirkby Stephen in Westmorland in severe turbulance near high ground. Baled out and landed safely with sprained ankle. Aircraft written off.

3 July 49

PII R A Bailey of No 611 Squadron spun in on glide approach on return from Exercise Foil at Coltishall, crashed into grounds of St Georges Approved Schol, Formby. Pilot killed instantly, Spitfire PK521 burned out.

11 June50

Pilot II Peter Lowthian of 611 Squadron touched wings with 613 Squadron aircraft whilst practice formation flying at Biggin Hill. Tail chopped off and aircraft crashed, pilot killed instantly. Spitfire XXII PK322.

14 December 51

Chipmunk T10 WB552 of University of Liverpool Air Squadron crash-landed in practice forced-landing area when engine failed to pick up. Crew OK.

4 May 52

Fg Off K G S Hargreaves RAFVR, commander of the THUM Flight killed in Spitfire PR19 PM549 on approach in bad weather and with radio failure. Aircraft spun whilst turning onto finals.

20 December 52

Fg Off Limpett-Low of 19 Reserve Flying School crash-landed in Chipmunk T10 south of Formby after carb icing. Aircraft written off, pilot OK.

27 June53

Chipmunk T10 WD326 of Manchester University Air Squadron crashed at Waltham Moor, Near Skipton killing Fg Off K B Wallace and Plt Off F Reddish.

4 March 54

Flt Lt Tommy Heyes RAFVR killed in Spitfire PR19 PM628 at Church Pulverback, Salop in crash landing after engine failure on routine Thum Flight met climb. Plaque in church dedicated by his wife, Iris and friends. Aircraft written off.

14 April 54

Spitfire PR19 PM651 force-landed at Halfpenny Green after engine overspeeding and low oil pressure on routine THUM climb. Aircraft not re-issued for flying duties, being delivered to Rolls Royce at Hucknall for display purposes. Pilot, John Formby, unhurt.

22 July 54

Spitfire PR19 PS853 of the THUM Flight force-landed at the disused airfield at Calveley, Cheshire due to carburettor problems. After repair, flown back to Woodvale. Pilot OK.

24 December 54

Spitfire PR19 PS915 force-landed at Woodvale after canopy disintergrated at 30,000 ft. Pilot, John Formby, eventually recovered control and landed, very cold, safely at Woodvale.

1 January 55

Spitfire PR19 PM652 of the Thum Flight crashed near RAF High Ercall, Salop after throwing con-rod on ferry trip from RAF Colerne to Woodvale. Written off in belly landing. Pilot John Formby not hurt.

15 April 56

Sqn Ldr L J Cook of Liverpool UAS killed in Chipmunk T10 WD 351 at Lydiate. Passenger received slight injuries.

The remains of Chipmunk WD351/U of Liverpool UAS after a fatal crash at Lydiate, 5 miles east of the airfield on 15 April 1956.   *C.J. Foulds*

12 June 57

Spitfire PRXIX PS853 suffered engine failure just after take-off on last flight from Woodvale. During subsequent forced-landing aircraft tipped onto its nose. Superficial damage to aircraft. Pilot, John Formby, unhurt.

A rearward view of Spitfire PR XIX PS853 after tipping on its nose after an aborted take off on 12 June 1957.   *John Formby*

23 October 57

Mosquito T35 TK604/Q written off in belly landing at Woodvale after wheels would not lock down. Pilot, Eric Richards of the Thum Flight flew over beach to jettison winch. Winch failed to separate, pilot unaware but due to slow running, one engine failed and aircraft landed on winch.

22 December 65

Chipmunk T10 WP968 of MUAS crashed into Winter Hill and was written off, crew OK.

22 July 76

Two Bulldog T1(s (XX632/F and ?) of Yorkshire UAS, Leeming, on summer camp at Woodvale crashed on Ainsdale Beach. Sqn Ldr George Dunn (34) injured back, Flt Lt David Sergeant (32) and Cadet Pilots Martin Brown and Tony Atkinson (both 29) minor injuries. Both aircraft written-off.

Bulldog T1 XX6 of Yorks UAS on Ainsdale Beach on 22 July 1976 after failing to recover from a spin. Both crew escaped but one suffered back injuries due to abandoning the aircraft at low level and his parachute only just deploying before he landed.   *Visitor Series of Newspapers*

2 March 88

Acting Plt Off Mark F Davies (20) killed in Bulldog T1, XX712 of MASUAS after crash-landing on beach at Southport. Spun after unauthorised low flying. Aircraft written-off.

19 July 88

Bulldog T1, XX630/A of Liverpool UAS force-landed on Pakefield beach, near Lowestoft after engine failure. Removed by helicopter. Pilot, Flt Lt "Paddy" Cooney OK. Squadron on summer camp at RAF West Raynham. Pilot received Green Endorsement.

Representative Aircraft

308 Squadron	Spitfire II	P7745 P8022 P8089 P8147 P8087 P8142 P8147 P7501 P8206 P8475
	Spitfire Vb	P8746 W3825 W3932 AB202
315 Squadron	Spitfire Vb	W3764 W3618 AB241 AB931 AB898 BL751 AB230 AB215 AB231 W3507 AB895 BL959
776 Squadron	Chesapeake I	AL950 AL919 AL918 AL947 AL944 AL951 AL930 AL946
	Skua	L3004 L2971 L4014 L2908 L3045 L2977 L2936 L2879
	Roc	L3164 L3175 L3160 L3167 L3087 L3192 L3075
	Dominie	X5708
256 Squadron	Beaufighter I	X7845
	Beaufighter If	R2069 R2091 R2207 R2247
	Beaufighter VIf	V8434 V8443 V8457 V8458 V8460 V8470 V8472 V8489 V8490 V8497 V8499 V8501
317 Squadron	Spitfire Vb	BM422 W3375 AB866 AA929 BL238 AA943 AB914 W3507 ED230 EN856 BM597 AR431 AD262 W3507 BM567 AB241
116 Squadron	Oxford	R5974 BG628
195 Squadron	Typhoon IB	EJ909 DN331 DN266 DN424 DN304 DN389 DN412 DN314 DN328 DN373 R8938 R7914 EJ909 EJ915 EJ910
	Hurricane	V7778 ?2427
	Tiger Moth	??209
198 Squadron	Typhoon IB	DN249 DN299 DN302 DN304 DN306 DN314
285 Squadron	Defiant TT.1	N1553 T3923 N1610 V1134 N1706 DR882
	Oxford	X7280 HM833 LX640 LX641 LX643 LX464 LX462 HM731 HM703 HM846 LX624 HM908
	Martinet	MS507
	Beaufighter If	X7550 R2076 T4640 X7712
	Hurricane IV	LE508
	Hurricane IIC	LF600 LF646 LF623 LF688
222 Squadron	Spitfire IX	MH371
	Spitfire LFIX	MH430 MH423 MH416 MH434 MH476 MH439 MH491 MH428
12 (P) Advanced Flying Unit	Blenheim I	L1194 K7175 K7089 L6751
	Blenheim IV	Z5807
	Blenheim V	AZ957 BA783 AZ884 BA164 BA104 AZ877 AZ988 AZ900 AZ957 AZ948 BA147
650 Squadron	Hurricane	LE757 KZ911
577 Squadron	Hurricane IIC	LF692 LF652
	Vengeance II	HB424 HB494
611 Squadron	Spitfire XIV	FM814 NH702 NH707 NH784 NM814 NM816 MV303 MV309 RB165 RM794 RM824 RN210 SM886 TZ139 TZ141
	Harvard IIB	KF223 KF225 KF640 KF373
	Spitfire XXII	PK322 PK481 PK485 PK381 PK521 PK540 PK552 PK632 PK650 PK652 PK659 PK669 PK675 PK381 PK520 PK631 PK606 (For 12 Group liaison work)
	Meteor F4	VW257 VT121 VT187 VW287 VT294 RA456 VW276
	Meteor T7	WF779 WA743
	Oxford	V4102

A 611 Squadron Harvard undergoing servicing whilst at summer camp at Tangmere in 1948. *611 Squadron collection*

A 611 Squadron Spitfire FXXII at Woodvale in 1950. *611 Squadron collection*

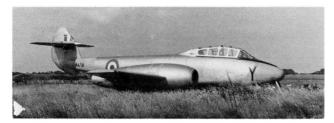

Although not on the strength of 611 Squadron at Woodvale, this Meteor T7 WA718 saw service with 611 Squadron at Hooton Park and ended its days as a fire practice wreck at Woodvale. Seen here just after its arrival in August 1968 before being slowly wrecked. *APF*

WA 718 seen in June 1970 in a dispersal near the railway line in a state of decay. *APF*

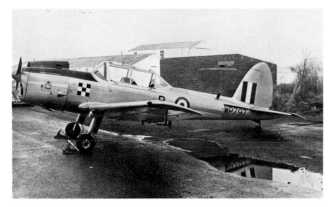

Chipmunk T10 WP797 parked in front of the maintenance Hangar – October 1968. *APF*

Bulldog XX688/S of LUAS October 1988. *APF*

186 Gliding School	Schneider Grunan Baby II	VT919
	Cadet TX.1	RA844 RA905 VM681 VM518
	Sedburgh TX.1	WB928 WB986 WB926
University of Liverpool Air Squadron	Chipmunk T10	WB697 WB760 WD289 WD351 WD352 WD375 WD365 WG300 WK555 WK590 WK631 WK643 WP788 WP797 WP857 WP980 WP929 WP973 WZ846 WB552 WK355
	Bulldog T1	XX630 XX678 XX685 XX686 XX688 XX687 XX712
19 Reserve Flying School	Chipmunk T10	WB710 WB775 WD308 WD309 WD310 WD318 WD319 WD320 WD323 WG460 WG471 WG775 WG914 WK643 WP471 WP550 WP775 WP782 WP829 WP909 WP914 WP919 WP829 WB649 WD307 WG319
	Tiger Moth	R5243 R5243 T6063 T6121 T7071 T7397
	Oxford	HM973 LW815 NJ303 W6626 LW815 HN309 AT778 ??231 ??230
	Anson XXI	VM510 VP523 VV305 VV316 VV324 VV326 VV330 VV361 VV897 VV913 VV917 VV919 VV982 VV999 WB452 WG515 WJ515 ??550
	Harvard	FT208 KF255
	Provost T1	XF610 XF684 XF836 XF838 XF839 XF887 XF888 XF889

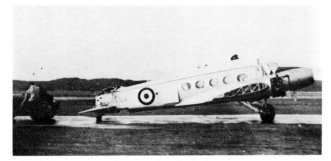

Anson XX1 VV324 of 19 RFS being towed to a disposal for burning after being stripped of its useful equipment (including engines) it was burned with Mosquito TK604 in January 1958 *C.J. Foulds*

Spitfire PRXIX PS 853 landing on runway 04 in 1957 with John Formby at the controls. The Old Golf Club House, used as a war-time Officers' Mess for several months, can be seen in the background. *F. Chapman*

THUM Flight	Spitfire PR19	PM577 PM628 PM631 PM651 PS853 PS915
	Spitfire 24	VN315
	Mosquito TT35	??303 RS719 TA641 TA722 TK604 TJ138 VR806
Civilian Fighter	Oxford I	DF231 HM973 LB468 NJ303
Control Co-op Unit	HN309 LX693	
	Provost T1	XF836 XF839 XF684 XF890
Manchester	Chipmunk T10	WD322 WD900 WP912 WB739 WD390 WK639 WP841
University	Bulldog	XX549 XX614 XX615 XX616 XX617 XX668 XX710
Air Squadron		
Western Sector	Oxford I	NJ305
Flight	Meteor F8	WA844 WK807
	Anson C19	VL349
	Anson T.21	VV349 VV882

Mosquito TT35 of the Thum Flight June 1957.　　*Visitor Series of Newspapers*

Chipmunk T10 WG422 of MUAS in October 1968 wearing the old Squadron markings.　　*APF*

Chipmunk T10 WP900 of MUAS in February 1971 in modified markings incorporating the units badge.　　*APF*

Bulldog T1 XX616/3 of MASUAS in the refurbished hangar in March 1991.　　*APF*

Meteor F8 WK884 was utilised by Western Sector Flight and No. 5 CAACU seen here taxi-ing out in 1960.

No 5 C A A C U	Mosquito TT35	TA722 VR806
	Meteor T7	WG984 WF784 WH166 WF791
	F8	VZ508 WH303 WH493 WK914 WK884 WH453 VZ540 WF711 VZ493
	TT20	WM224 WD646
No 10 Air Experience Flight	Chipmunk T10	WK522 WP555 WP786 WP789 WP870 WP973 WK624 WP896 WP786 WP900 WK639 WP984 WP551 WB654

Busy line up on the North Dispersal area showing two Mosquitoes TT35's (VR806/J in foreground) and four Meteors of No. 5 CAACU beyond. Photo probably taken in 1959.

Meteor T7 WF791 of No. 5 CAACU parked on a sunny afternoon in November 1966. *APF*

Meteor F8 VZ493/0 in 1960. This aircraft belonged to No. 5 CAACU.

Chipmunk T10 WK624/12 of 10 AEF in the 'Meteor' Hangar in June 1987. *APF*

Graves Relating to RAF Woodvale

OUR LADY OF COMPASSION CHURCH, SCHOOL LANE, FORMBY

Flying Officer E Krawczynski	308 Squadron	21 December 1941
Squadron Leader M J Wesolowski	308 Squadron	9 January 1941
Pilot Officer T T Nawrocki	315 Squadron	19 July 1942
Por F Fiedorczuk	315 Squadron	15 August 1942
Flying Officer B J Sawiak	315 squadron	23 August 1942

ST PETER'S CHURCH, GREEN LANE, FORMBY

Sergeant Pilot W A Dixon	195 Squadron	9 April 1943

LYTHAM ST ANNE'S, LANCASHIRE

Pilot Officer R R Walters	198 Squadron	26 May 1943

THORNTON CLEVELEYS, BLACKPOOL

Flying Officer R I Reid	602 Squadron	31 July 1947

The four Polish graves at Our Lady's Church, Formby, containing five dead from RAF Woodvale.   *APF*

AIRFIELD DESCRIPTION

1944   Fighter Command (No 9 Group)

Three runways   22/04   4,816 feet   by   156 feet   2 inches
                       17/35   3,287 feet   by   155 feet   7 inches
                       09/27   3,505 feet   by   157 feet   0 inches

Hangars   Three of Bellman type
                       Nine extra-over Blisters

Hardstandings   12 double for twin engined aircraft (24)
                       10 for single engined aircraft

Lighting   Mk II Lighting - Drem and portable goose-neck flares

Radio   VHF only

Sites   Main Site (Airfield)
                       Defence Site
                       Communal Site
                       Sick Quarters Site
                       Seven Airmen's Living Sites
                       WAAF Communal Site
                       One WAAF Living Site
                       Operations Block
                       Two W/T Sites

1991   Support Command (RAF College Cranwell)

Three Runways   22/04   6,001 feet/1,829m   Asphalt
                       17/35   3,287 feet/1,002m   Asphalt
                       09/27   3,463 feet/1,056m   Asphalt

Hangars   Two of Bellman type

Hardstanding   One on site of No 1 Hangar - concrete.
                       One on site in front of RAF hangar − brick paving

Lighting   High Intensity Sodium on threshold to 22.
                       Portable runway lamps.
                       Portable taxiway lights

Radio   VHF − tower
                       UHF − tower
                       UHF/DF

Site   Main Site only

Elevation   37 feet AMSL

Beacon   Portable electric beacon flashing "WV" in red

Gate Guardian

Gloster Meteor T7 WA591 has been "On Guard" on the main gate at Woodvale just outside the Officers' Mess for seven years, after a lengthy refurbishment and protection from the local salty air. It is the first gate guard ever to be positioned at Woodvale and depicts the association with Meteors of No 611 (West Lancs) Squadron Royal Auxiliary Air Force and those of No 5 Civilian Anti-Aircraft Co-Operation Unit which operated for many years from the airfield.

It was built at the Gloster Aircraft Company factory at Hucclecote, Gloucestershire, as part of Contract No 6/ACFT/2982 CB 7(B) dated 25 November 1948 for the first production batch of T Mk 7s amounting to 137 aircraft. Awaiting collection at Hucclecote on 28 April 1949 it was issued to the Central Fighter establishment at RAF West Raynham, Norfolk, on 2 September 1949. A move to No 226 Operational Conversion Unit at RAF Stradishall, Suffolk, took place on 31 October 1949, followed by No 203 Advanced Flying School at RAF Driffield, Yorks, on 20 November 1950 and No 208 Advanced Flying School at RAF Merryfield, Somerset, on 15 May 1952 and on to No 215 Advanced Flying School at RAF Finningley on 10 March 1953.

WA591 had several flying accidents, one on 6 August 1953 put it back to Glosters and on to No 33 Maintenance Unit at RAF Lyneham, Wilts, after repair on 2 July 1954. From here it went to No 12 Flying Training School at RAF Weston Zoyland, Somerset, on 9 December 1954. From here it went to No 38 Maintenance Unit at RAF Llandow, South Wales. It then moved on to Avro's for a refurbish during early 1956 moving back to No 12 Maintenance Unit at RAF Kirkbride on 26 July 1956, going back to No 33 Maintenance Unit on 16 March 1959. It joined the College of Air Warfare at RAF Manby, Lincs, on 29 June 1959; No 5 Maintenance Unit at RAF Kemble, Gloucs, on 30 August 1961 and back to No 33 Maintenance Unit again on 12 October 1961. On 25 January 1962 it was alloted to No 5 Flying Training School at RAF Oakington, Cambs, transferring to No 8 Flying Training School at RAF Driffield, Yorks, on 24 February 1962 and back to the College of Air Warfare at RAF Manby on 13 August 1962.

Its last accident was on 11 July 1963, to Category 3 (aircraft damaged, repair on site possible, but not by operating unit), the repairs being carried out by a team from No 60 Maintenance Unit, based at RAF Dishforth, Yorks, by 29 August. It was retired to No 5 Maintenance Unit at RAF Kemble on 4 May 1965 and declared a non-effective airframe on 23 July 1965. Escaping the scrap-mans axe, it joined the No 5 Maintenance Unit Apprentice School as 7917 M on 16 August 1966, moving to the Civilian Craft Apprentice School at RAF St Athan during the early 1970s. It was declared redundant at RAF St Athan in 1978 and was allocated to RAF Woodvale for display purposes. It arrived by road at RAF Woodvale on 8 December 1978. It was assembled in the maintenance hangar and slowly refurbished by students from the University Air Squadrons until a team arrived from RAF St Athan to place it onto purpose built legs just inside the main gate. Unfortunately its attitude steepened when some students staged a tea-party on the tail-plane causing the concrete block to rise under the nose wheel.

Today it reminds passing motorists of the function of RAF Woodvale – training and support.

The Meteor being erected at the gate by a crew from RAF St Athan in September 1983. *Squadron Leader Cliff Hilliker*

Meteor T7 WA591 'on guard' at the main gate June 1991.

APF

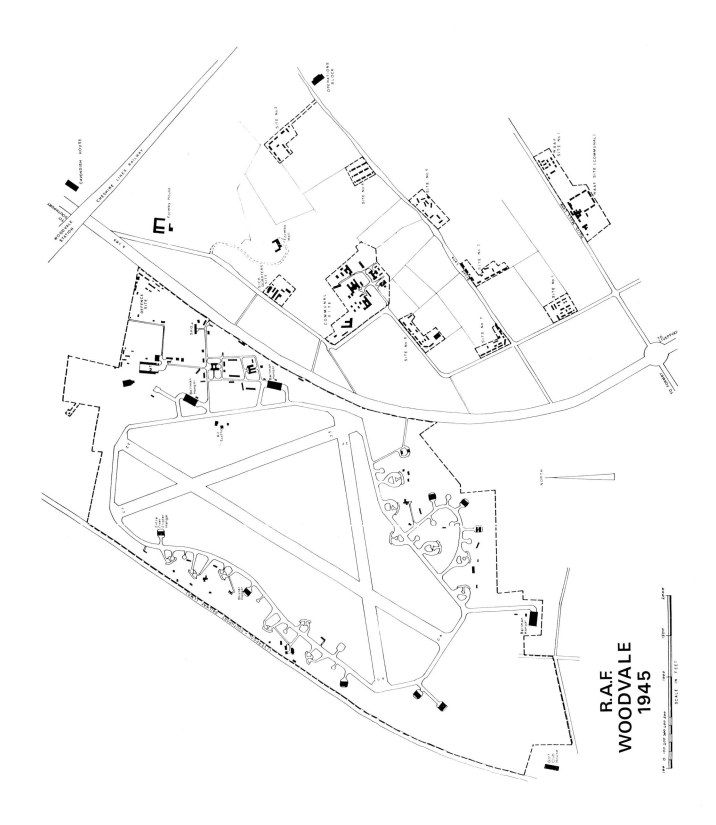

R.A.F.
WOODVALE
1945

SCALE IN FEET

NORTH

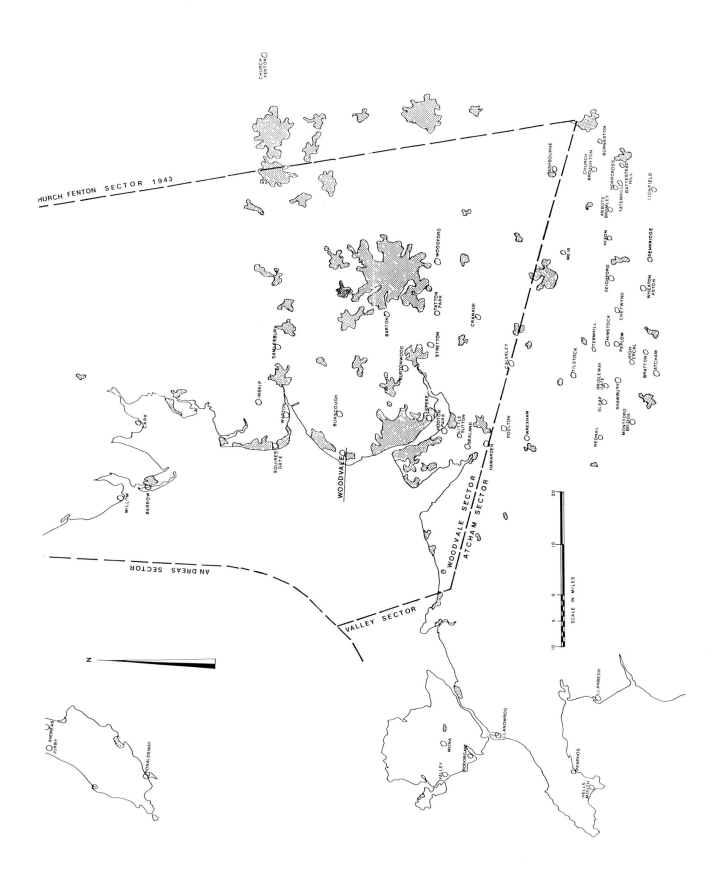

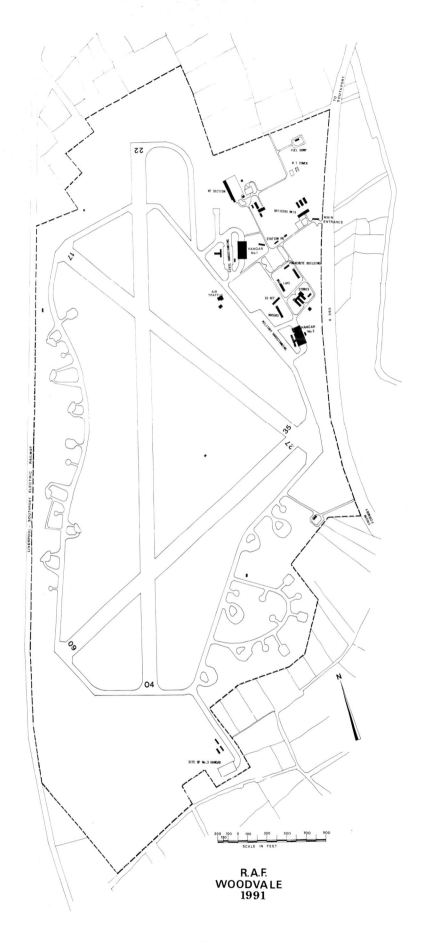

R.A.F.
WOODVALE
1991

Original main guardroom at the Main Entrance where it has always stood. Originally containing cells and a police dog compound and kennels to the rear, these have now been demolished. Seen here in January 1974 before the buildings were 'toned down' with green painted exteriors. *APF*

Since 1974 the guardroom has recieved new windows and a porch for all weather protection and new gates with automatic traffic barriers installed. Pictured in June 1991. *APF*

The domestic fire station stood by the main gate, opposite to the guardroom until 1988 when it was demolished. Pictured in June 1985. *APF*

Station Headquarters moved to this building in 1961 when the current Officers' Mess was opened and the administrative function moved here. This photograph taken in June 1985 shows it before it was re-roofed and totally refurbished . *APF*

Originally the Station Headquarters, the Officers' Mess was converted and extended in 1960/61 with the new kitchens added to the far end and three sleeping annexes (Vulcan, Victor and Valiant) added to the rear. The extension at this end of the buildings was added in the 1980's as an extension to the anti-room and bar. *APF*

Station Workshops stood until about 1986. This building provided the engineering support for the entire station from 1942 to 1956 when the workshops alongside the Maintenance Hangar were constructed. Little used after that date it fell into disrepair and was demolished in 1986. The unloading ramp which can be seen is all that remains today. *APF*

The Parachute Packing Building with its unusual roof for the hanging of parachutes as it was in 1974. It has since been totally cladded in steel to waterproof the original single brick thick walls and improve insulation. The station workshops can be seen to the right. *APF*

The Parachute Building as it appears in March 1991 with its new external cladding. The station workshops have by now been demolished (to the right). *APF*

Originally built as a Squadron Office and used by many of the fighter Squadrons during the war and later by 611 and 2611 Squadrons, this building was the home of MUAS (later MASUAS) for many years until demolished in 1989 and the site used for a new prefabricated building now the HQ of LUAS. Photographed June 1985. *APF*

Liverpool University Air Squadron occupied this site since arriving at Woodvale in 1951 although the newer building was a much more recent addition. Since LUAS moved to their new building this is now occupied by Woodvale Aviation Ltd. Photo June 1985. *APF*

The site of the previous photo is now occupied (1991) by a prefabricated building which is the HQ of LUAS. *APF*

Designed as the Link Trainer Building containing two trainers, 10AEF occupied this building from 1958. Moving out to an inferior prefabricated building in the early 1980's. West Lancs Aero Club took it over and have substantially modified and improved it since. Photographed in February 1982. *APF*

Also built as a Squadron Office this was the office building for the civilian contractor giving ground support at Woodvale. Originally Short Bros. & Harland, then Airwork Services and several others including Marshalls of Cambridge and CSE Ltd. It was demolished in 1979 and the base used for the new HQ of MASUAS. *APF*

10AEF moved into this smaller building for several years waiting for their new HQ to be completed. It is now the home of 611 Squadron Air Training Corps who had to vacate the old armoury building when it was demolished. Photo 1985. *APF*

The new MASUAS HQ on the site of the old contractors office building. March 1991. *APF*

10AEF occupy this superb new HQ after suffering for several years in a much smaller building. This site was the station armoury occupied until 1990 by 1430 later 611 Squadron ATC. *APF*

The inside of the original Maintenance hangar in 1991 having been totally reclad and re-roofed, new lights and heating and the hangar now used by the RAF for their Chipmunks and Bulldogs. *APF*

The 'Meteor Bellman type hangar was constructed in 1951 alongside the lower hangar of the same type originally built in 1940. This hangar was required for the larger Meteor which were joining No. 611 Squadron. Vacated by the RAF in 1990 it is now occupied by the civilian flying organisation. *APF*

Now totally refurbished the original Maintenance hangar as it looked in 1985. The boiler house and offices were added in about 1956 to enhance the maintenance facilities and provide full heating. *APF*

The plan of the airfield was rendered over in the 1950's and not rediscovered until 1975 when refurbishment work uncovered it. It was fully re-instated using war-time photos supplied by the author and is thought unique today still depicting its war-time map. *APF*

The Control Tower is usually the focal centre of an airfield and the Woodvale Tower was built to standard drawing No. 12779/41 but locally modified to drawing No. W/614/41. Seen here in August 1947 it is in exactly the same format as it was constructed in 1941 with the timber and glass 'Local Control' greenhouse on top. Summer temperatures were unbearable inside! The original New Bronk Farm House can be seen to the right of the tower behind Puss Moth G-AIPH operated by the Southport Aero Club. *Dave Vernon*

By 1971 the farm house had long since been demolished. The primary glider was owned by St Mary's School, Crosby CCF and was used for filming a Blue Peter BBC programme in January 1971.
APF

The interim Control Room was a failure due to its vertical windows. Seen here in January 1979.
APF

The tower as it now stands in toned-down green.
APF

In the 1970's a new Local Control was added to Woodvale's tower but was not successful and was replaced with the current control room in 1980. Taken in January 1980 the new outward sloping windows are visible plus the ground floor sideways extension and the fire section to the left. Whilst the tower was out of operation a mobile control tower was utilised for Air Traffic purposes.
APF

The rear of the tower taken in 1987 showing the fully refurbished plan – omitting the extension to 04/22 and new external escape stairs and communicating mast.
APF

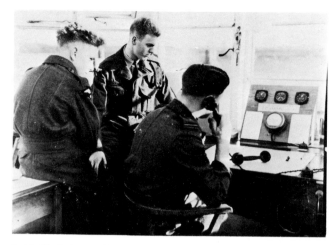

Inside Woodvale control tower circa 1949.   *611 Squadron collection*

Up to date internal view showing excellent visibility with the local controller sitting with the approach controller standing.   *Trinity Weekly Newspapers*

The Approach Controllers position with screen for Direction Finding on the right (RDF). The Local Controller sits to the left − off the picture. Note the original timber framed small glass structure. Photo approx 1955.

Mrs Brenda Youlton

LUAS depicts their badge of the Liver Bird on the book of learning with seaweed in its mouth. Chipmunk May 1970.   *APF*

LUAS markings (vandalised by a Royal Navy Linx Flight) as worn today on each side of the Bulldog fuselage. March 1991.   *APF*

Markings applied to 10AEF Chipmunks show the red rose of Lancashire with '10' in the middle with two 'local' seagulls above 1991.   *APF*

MUAS marking on a Chipmunk in May 1970.   *APF*

The badge of MUAS on the side of a Squadron Bulldog aircraft.   *APF*

ABOUT THE
AUTHOR

Born to parents from Southport, Aldon Patrick Ferguson was born in Epping, Essex (within sight of North Weald Fighter Airfield) in August 1945. After the end of the War the family returned to Merseyside, settling in Freshfield near Formby within a few hundred yards of the perimeter of RAF Woodvale. Interest in aviation was fed by the proximity of Woodvale, and Aldon joined the Air Training Corps there, being a founder member of 1430 (Formby) Squadron based on Woodvale itself and eventually gained a commission with the RAFVR(T).

Educated at Merchant Taylors, Crosby and the Liverpool College of Building he took up surveying as a career. After a short period in the RAF he joined a Liverpool firm of estate agents and moved to London in 1976. He is now senior partner of his own firm of chartered surveyors and commercial property consultants dealing with properties not only throughout the UK but in Eastern Europe and the USSR.

Eventually gaining a Private Pilots Licence, first soloing at Woodvale with the West Lancs Aero Club, frustration of a non-flying career was partly overcome. Aldon's interest in airfield histories, kindled by Woodvale, has led to several books and many magazines articles, together with editorship of the magazine of the Airfield Research Group. Now living in Wargrave, Reading with his wife, Sue, Aldon still manages to monitor developments at Woodvale and run the Burtonwood Association (product of his two books on that Station). Aldon's mother still lives in Southport and he has a sister and two brothers.

Front Cover
The Red Arrows, the RAF's official aerobatic team opening their display at Woodvale in April 1973. Note that they were flying Hawker Siddeley Gnat Aircraft at the time. *Stephenson Newspapers*

Back Cover.
A superb formation of MUAS Bulldogs seen in the blue sky over Woodvale in 1990. *Squadron Leader Rod Newman*